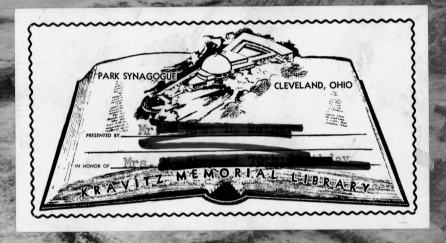

# PROPHETS, IDOLS
*and*
# DIGGERS

THE SILVER CHALICE

# PROPHETS, IDOLS

## AND

# DIGGERS

## Scientific Proof of Bible History

by

JOHN ELDER

THE **BOBBS-MERRILL** COMPANY, INC.
A SUBSIDIARY OF HOWARD W. SAMS & CO., INC.
Publishers · INDIANAPOLIS · NEW YORK

Grateful acknowledgment is made to the following authors and publishers for permission to reprint or paraphrase material which is in copyright or of which they are the authorized publishers:

To the American Sunday-School Union: quotations from G. A. Barton's *Archaeology and the Bible* (1916). Used by permission.

To Dodd, Mead & Company: Reprinted by permission of Dodd, Mead & Company, Inc. from *In the Steps of the Master* by H. V. Morton. Copyright 1934 by Dodd, Mead & Company, Inc.

To Doubleday & Company, Inc.: quotations from the introduction to W. F. Albright's *From the Stone Age to Christianity* (Doubleday-Anchor Books edition, 1957). Used by permission.

To Eyre & Spottiswoode, Ltd.: quotations from Sir Charles Marston's *The Bible Comes Alive* (1937). Used by permission.

To Farrar, Straus & Cudahy, Inc.: quotations from Nelson Glueck's *Rivers in the Desert* (1959). Used by permission.

To Hodder & Stoughton, Ltd.: quotations from Sir George Adam Smith's *Historical Geography of the Holy Land* (1920). Used by permission.

To Johns Hopkins Press: quotations from W. F. Albright's *Archaeology and the Religion of Israel* (1942). Used by permission.

To Alfred A. Knopf, Inc.: quotations from C. W. Ceram's *Gods, Graves and Scholars* (1951). Used by permission.

To Princeton University Press: quotations from Jack Finegan's *Light from the Ancient Past* (1946) and J. B. Pritchard's *Ancient Near Eastern Texts Relating to the Old Testament* (1950). Used by permission.

To Fleming H. Revell Company: quotations from Sir Charles Marston's *The Bible Comes Alive* (1938). Used by permission.

To Charles Scribner's Sons: quotations from Sir C. Leonard Woolley's *Ur of the Chaldees* (1930) and Henry Van Dyke's *The Toiling of Felix and Other Poems* (1900) and *Out-of-Doors in the Holy Land* (1908). Used by permission.

To The Westminster Press: a passage paraphrased from George E. Wright's *Biblical Archaeology* (1957). Used by permission.

## *To RUTH*

For whither thou goest, I will go; and where
   thou lodgest, I will lodge: thy people
   shall be my people, and thy God my God.

Where thou diest, will I die, and there will
   I be buried: the Lord do so to me, and more
   also, if ought but death part thee and me.

# FOREWORD

IN THE SPRING OF 1919, IN THE NEWLY FORMED REPUBLIC OF AZER-
BAIJAN, I visited on the edge of the town of Nakhichevan the tomb
said to have been that of the patriarch Noah. When I asked my
guide how he knew it was Noah's tomb, he answered in some surprise: "I live here, of course I know it."

Perhaps it was his somewhat unsatisfactory reply that awakened
in me an interest in archeology that has continued to grow during
my period of residence in the Near East. I lived for some years in
Kermanshah, six miles from the remarkable Sassanian carvings of
Tak-i Bustan, and for a time in Hamadan, built squarely atop the
former Achaemenian city of Ecbatana. For the past twenty years
I have lived in Tehran, some six miles from the ruins of the storied
city of Rei or Rhagae. The opportunities given me to explore the
ruins have served to deepen my interest in the lives and works of
ancient peoples.

It was with genuine pleasure that I accepted an invitation from
a group of Europeans and Americans living in Tehran to lead them
in a study of Biblical archeology. Reading up for these lectures
was for me a delight and a stimulus, while the sustained interest of
those who enthusiastically supported the meetings has been a recurring inspiration. Inevitably, the materials included in my lectures
were drawn from the writings of others, so it is the purpose of this
Foreword to acknowledge my debt and to introduce to you who
read this book some of the authoritative volumes which concern
this fascinating subject.

7

Several books dealing with the entire span of Biblical history have been constantly before me. One of the richest·sources has been *Light from the Ancient Past*, by Jack Finegan (Princeton: Princeton University Press, 1946). Equally valuable has been the revised edition of *The Westminster Historical Atlas to the Bible*, by G. E. Wright and Floyd V. Filson (Philadelphia: Westminster Press, 1956). To these must be added G. E. Wright's splendidly illustrated book, *Biblical Archaeology* (Philadelphia: Westminster Press, 1957). *Archaeology and the Bible*, by George A. Barton (Philadelphia: American Sunday-School Union, 1916), is a mine of information, though some of its material is somewhat out of date. Barton's book is of particular value for its translations of such documents as the Code of Hammurabi, Hittite and Assyrian law codes and the texts of many important papyri. Another most authoritative writer is William Foxwell Albright, whose books *From the Stone Age to Christianity* (Baltimore: Johns Hopkins Press, 1940), also available in a Doubleday-Anchor Books edition, *The Archaeology of Palestine* (Baltimore: Penguin Books Inc., 1951), *Archaeology and the Religion of Israel* (Baltimore: Johns Hopkins Press, 1942), *The Bible After Twenty Years of Archaeology* (Biblical Colloquium, 1954) and *Recent Discoveries in Bible Lands* (Biblical Colloquium, 1955) are reliable and informative.

For information concerning archeology and the Old Testament, I recommend the revised edition of *The Monuments and the Old Testament*, by Ira M. Price (Philadelphia: Judson Press, 1958), on which I have relied for information regarding Old Testament discoveries. In the following pages I have drawn upon J. B. Pritchard's authoritative work, *Ancient Near Eastern Texts Relating to the Old Testament* (Princeton: Princeton University Press, 2nd ed., 1950) for quotations pertaining to Mesopotamian historical and mythological literature. Sir Charles Marston's *New Bible Evidence* (Westwood, New Jersey: Revell, 1934) is entertaining reading but to be checked against more scholarly accounts. C. W. Ceram's *Gods, Graves and Scholars* (New York: Alfred Knopf, 1951) has some interesting chapters on excavations in the Holy Land.

*Ancient Mesopotamia, A Light That Did Not Fail*, Ephraim A. Speiser's account of early Mesopotamian civilization first published as a beautifully illustrated brochure by the *National Geographic Magazine*, is authoritative for that era. For the civilization of Sumer, Sir Charles Leonard Woolley is an acknowledged authority. His earlier book, *The Sumerians* (Oxford: Clarendon Press, 1928), has been followed by *Excavations at Ur* (London: E. Benn, 1954). The brochure, *The Ras Shamra Tablets,* published by the University of Chicago, affords an excellent early study of the finds at Ras Shamra. Two books by S. M. Kramer, *From the Tablets of Sumer* (Indian Hills, Col.: Falcon's Wing Press, 1956) and *History Begins at Sumer* (London: Thames & Hudson, 1958), present his latest conclusions regarding the civilization of the Sumerians. *The History of Herodotus,* by George Rawlinson (New York: Tudor, 1943), has many fascinating but not always accurate stories of ancient Babylon and Persia.

A flood of recent books concern the Dead Sea scrolls, generally considered to be the most important manuscript finds of the century. Public attention was first captured by Edmund Wilson's long article in *The New Yorker* in May 1955. In August of the same year, *The Christian Century,* in a series of articles by Dr. Frank Cross, enlarged on and emendated Wilson's article. The best early account of these discoveries is Millar Burrows' *The Dead Sea Scrolls* (New York: Viking Press, 1955), a work which has since been brought up to date in Burrows' *More Light on the Dead Sea Scrolls* (New York: Viking Press, 1958). The texts of the Dead Sea scrolls, as deciphered through 1956, are paraphrased rather than translated in Theodor Gaster's *The Dead Sea Scriptures* (Garden City, N.Y.: Doubleday, 1956). Other important books on this subject are F. M. Cross's *The Ancient Library of Qumran and Modern Biblical Studies* and *The Scrolls and the New Testament* by Krister Stendahl (New York: Harper, 1957). Articles in the *Bulletin of the American Schools of Oriental Research* and the *Journal of Biblical Literature* and the *Biblical Archaeologist* continue to bring news of recent discoveries and translations.

For the New Testament period, Josephus' *Wars of the Jews* and *Antiquities of the Jews* are invaluable as contemporary accounts of Palestine as it was in the first century.

Two books by H. V. Morton, *In the Steps of the Master* (New York: Dodd, Mead, 1934) and *In the Steps of St. Paul* (New York: Dodd, Mead, 1936), are delightful and replete with archeological references, and I have referred to them often.

For the Jordan Valley and its environs, no book excels *The River Jordan,* by Nelson Glueck (Philadelphia: Westminster Press, 1946). Glueck is both a top-flight archeologist and a most accomplished writer. See also Glueck's *Rivers in the Desert* (New York: Farrar, Straus & Cudahy, 1959).

In following the journeys of St. Paul, I found Sir William Ramsey's book, *St. Paul, the Traveler and Roman Citizen* (New York: Putnam's Sons, 1908), most helpful. Although published over one hundred years ago, *The Life and Epistles of St. Paul,* by Conybeare and Howson (New York: Longmans, Brown, Green & Longmans, 1853) is of exceptional interest. These, of course, are in addition to the works by the various authors mentioned above who deal with the Bible in its entirety.

Repeatedly I referred for detailed information to *The Encyclopaedia Britannica* and *The New International Encyclopaedia.* The newly published *Twentieth-Century Encyclopaedia* has excellent articles on archeological subjects, and the older *Popular and Critical Bible Encyclopaedia* has been a constant source of information. The various volumes of the commentary, *The Interpreter's Bible* (Nashville: Abingdon Press, 1953) are replete with archeological references as well as much other valuable information. Most important, the source of sources has been *The Holy Bible* on which these other books have shed new light.

I owe a special debt to Dr. George M. Landes for his careful reading of this manuscript and his many valuable suggestions. In general I have adopted these suggestions, though in a few instances, on the theory that "where doctors disagree, the patient makes his own choice," I have followed the opinion of others. His assistance has been invaluable. I am most grateful also to the Reverend and Mrs. C. H. Allen for their assistance at a critical time. To Mrs. Frank Gurney, who spent many hours typing the manuscript, and to the members of the class whose encouragement has meant so much, I must give my special thanks.

My hope is that the reading of this very condensed survey will inspire many to turn to more comprehensive works and learn more of the new light that archeology sheds upon the Old Book.

JOHN ELDER

Tehran, Iran
August 1959

# CONTENTS

## CONTENTS—*continued*

# ILLUSTRATIONS

The photograph on the jacket is taken from the Tripylon Relief at Persepolis, showing Darius I (seated) and Xerxes. (*Courtesy of the Oriental Institute, University of Chicago.*)

The endpapers at the front of this book show the Canaanite Temple of the god Mekal (the fourteenth century B.C.), the oldest of no less than five temples discovered at Beisan in Palestine. (*Courtesy of the University of Pennsylvania.*)

The endpapers at the back are an aerial view of the great Ziggurat at Ur, dating from about 550 B.C. A "ziggurat," of which this is the most complete example yet excavated, was the central part of a Mesopotamian temple area. (*Courtesy of the University of Pennsylvania.*)

# PROPHETS, IDOLS
*and*
# DIGGERS

# INTRODUCTION

## THE METHODS OF
## BIBLICAL ARCHEOLOGY

WE OFTEN THINK OF THE EARLY DAYS OF AMERICAN INDEPENDENCE as being an age of Faith. Having in mind a picture of our fore-fathers, the Pilgrims, for example, with guns on their arms as they proceeded en masse to church, we assume that in the good old days, from 1620 on, everyone believed in God and no one was troubled with doubts. Thus it comes as a shock to find, on the contrary, that among educated people, the last decades of the eighteenth century were a time when scepticism and theism were so widely prevalent as to be nearly universal. During a period of four years, we learn, Dartmouth College graduated only one man who believed in God, and we find that the percentage of the population belonging to the churches was less than one sixth what it is today.

One reason for this scepticism was a general disbelief in the Bible. Most educated people, greatly influenced by French thought, considered the Bible a collection of myths and fables, quite devoid of historical foundation. It was felt that Christianity was no more than a primitive superstition. Widely accepted was Voltaire's confident prediction that in a hundred years Christianity would be a dead religion. Historians and scientists of the day knew nothing of the ancient civilizations of Babylon, Nineveh and Tyre; Biblical allusions to their greatness and glory were accounted legends, the boasting of primitive peoples who lived as nomads in a wilderness of desolation.

Christians had no answer to give the sceptics. Of course the orthodox insisted that the Bible must be true because it was the

17

word of God; but historians thought it could not be the word of God because it was so obviously a collection of fables. There was no meeting, no wish to have a meeting of minds. Some aspects of Christianity, it was maintained, were of value, whatever the inaccuracy of historical references in the Bible. The Golden Rule is golden. The ethical teachings of Jesus and Paul are challenging and inspiring. Prayer is of evident value to the spirit, and love for one's neighbor will continue to be extolled, if not practiced, whatever the Bible may be discovered to be. And faith in something greater than one's self is still found to be essential to great achievement. Thus, while ethical teachings of Christianity would continue to appeal in their own right, the heart of Christianity as a religion might not survive a demonstration that, in many instances, the Bible is of no historical value. The conception of God the Father, Who chose the Jewish people as a vehicle of His revelation, as One who sent the prophets to guide and to warn them, and One who fully revealed himself only in His Son, Jesus Christ, Who was crucified for our sins and rose again—this concept would be seen as myth.

"We love because He first loved us and gave His Son to be the propitiation for our sins"—would no longer be the most powerful precept to sacrificial living the world has ever known, but a dream, a baseless legend.

It is not too much to say that it was the rise of the science of archeology that broke the deadlock between historians and the orthodox Christian. Little by little, one city after another, one civilization after another, one culture after another, whose memories were enshrined only in the Bible, were restored to their proper places in ancient history by the studies of archeologists. In the following pages the outlines of this development will be given in some detail. The over-all result is indisputable. Forgotten cities have been found, the handiwork of vanished peoples has reappeared, contemporary records of Biblical events have been unearthed and the uniqueness of Biblical revelation has been emphasized by contrast and comparison to the newly understood religions of ancient peoples. Nowhere has archeological discovery refuted the Bible as history.

It is not to be thought that there was no interest in archeology until comparatively recent times. From tablets found in Iraq we learn that Ashurbanipal, the great warrior-king of Assyria who reigned in the seventh century B.C. (668–626), was proud of his ability to decipher ancient tablets and sent scribes all over his empire to copy important ancient documents and bring the copies to his library. The discovery of this library by Rassam in 1852 was one of the most valuable finds of the nineteenth century. In the sixth century B.C., Nabonidus, the last king of Babylon, developed a deep interest in archeology. He explored the ancient ziggurat at Ur, read the foundation records of early builders and carefully restored them, giving full credit to his predecessors. His daughter, the sister of Belshazzar, shared his interest and maintained a small archeological museum.

Unfortunately, the main motive of ancient diggers was loot rather than learning. Particularly in Egypt, where fantastic treasures were buried with their rulers, grave robbers discovered and appropriated most of these hidden spoils. As far back as the time of Ramses IX, a government commission appointed by him to investigate the situation reported that practically all the ancient graves had been looted, the bodies thrown out and precious jewelry and implements stolen.

In modern times, Napoleon of France was one of the first to launch a systematic study of ancient ruins. On his expedition to Egypt in 1798, he took with him a group of one hundred scientists, scholars and artists who wrote careful accounts of the marvels of ancient Egypt and made quantities of sketches and water colors. The publication of their findings by the French government created a sensation in learned circles and aroused an interest in the East that has never died. The most significant of finds for the future of archeology was the Rosetta Stone in 1799 with its trilingual inscription that opened the secrets of hieroglyphic writing. But in the main, Napoleon's entourage studied what remained above ground. The investigation of what lay beneath waited another day.

Early in the nineteenth century, the British resident of the East India Company living in Baghdad reported the existence of mounds in Mesopotamia which were evidently the ruins of ancient cities. It was his report which led to the later digs by Sir Austen H. Layard and Paul Botta that launched the enterprise of archeological excavation which was to prove so incredibly fruitful. The story of these excavations will be sketched in the following chapters. Here we will anticipate a bit by describing some of the techniques that have been developed over a period of a hundred years by archeologists of many nations.

The earliest digs were inevitably crude and destructive by modern standards, and their purpose largely a search for striking and unusual museum pieces. The importance of pieces of broken pottery was not realized, nor the necessity of meticulous records appreciated. Thus a great deal of immensely valuable information was lost forever. It soon became evident that the larger mounds represented a long series of cities which had been erected on the same spot, sometimes as many as a score of successive communities each built on the ruins of its predecessors, the whole often representing a period of thousands of years. Naturally the latest city was on top, but lower layers were not always found one below the other like a neat layer of cake. It often happened that one age would be represented by a small settlement on the middle of the mound while a subsequent city, spreading beyond the former limits, would leave ruins on the outer reaches of the mound lower than those of the earlier city. It has been a task of almost infinite care and patience to unscramble the jumbled evidence and determine the exact chronology and correct order of these many layers.

Truly scientific archeology may be said to have begun in 1890 when Dr. Flinders Petrie dug for six weeks at Tell el-Hesi in southern Judea and demonstrated that the ruins were composed of more or less regularly superimposed layers which could be dated (relatively) by a comparison of artifacts, particularly pottery. He showed how the chronology of a mound could be worked out by a comparison of the artifacts' evolving shapes and patterns over the centuries. And as records and samples accumulated it became possible to establish with considerable accuracy the dates of various artifacts. Many of the shapes and patterns were found to be prevalent over wide areas during certain periods; the introduction of new forms was linked with invasions and conquests.

Through the years, many new inventions and discoveries have proved of great value to the archeologist. The invention of the camera gave him an invaluable tool, enabling him to photograph each find *in situ* before removing it to dig still deeper; and providing an accurate and permanent record of successive strata. The airplane has contributed its bit by revealing the outlines of forts and cities clearly visible from the air but unnoticeable to those on the ground. The X ray, used in examining mummified remains, makes it possible to discover the cause of death as well as the age and sex of the deceased. Infrared rays have been found effective in bringing out almost illegible writing on ancient manuscripts, and chemical tests and treatments have proved of similar value. One of the most recent tools of the archeologist is the carbon-14 test. A certain amount of the carbon in all living things is carbon 14 rather than the usual carbon 12. Carbon 14 is like radium in that it is unstable, throwing off tiny particles and slowly changing to carbon 12. This disintegration commences when the living host dies. By measuring the rate of disintegration a fairly accurate estimate can be made as to the time of death, an estimate that has been confirmed when remains already accurately dated have been submitted to this test. In short, almost every resource of modern science can be called upon to clarify our picture of ancient times. So successful have archeologists been that there is now a vast quantity of unstudied materials on hand; many years will be needed for thorough investigation.

*Courtesy of the University of Pennsylvania; from Collections in
the University Museum, Philadelphia*

CYLINDRICAL SEAL IMPRESSIONS, BABYLONIA

# I

# EARLY PIONEERS

BECAUSE OF ITS UNIQUE PLACE IN THE AFFECTIONS OF CHRISTIANS AND Jews alike, Palestine has for centuries been visited by scholars and pilgrims who in works of varying merit reported their impressions. One, like the German physician Rauchwolff, investigated the natural history and botany of the land; another, like Pietro della Valle, explored the ruins of ancient cities; Bishop Pococke drew many plans of the ruins and made copies of inscriptions; and Adrian Reland collected and studied all information then available (1709). But in 1838 an epoch-making exploration of Palestine was made, with the results considered revolutionary in the study of geography, topography and archeological remains. At this time the American theologian Dr. Edward Robinson, in company with his pupil, the Arabic-speaking missionary Eli Smith, spent some seven months traveling the length and breadth of Palestine and described and mapped several hundred Biblical sites and towns. However, the work accomplished by Robinson was almost entirely surface exploration.

The first pioneer in excavation whose work impinged directly on the field of Biblical archeology was Paul Botta, who in 1842 was appointed French consul in Mosul on the upper reaches of the Tigris River. From his first arrival Botta let it be known that he was ready to purchase antique objects of the type that occasionally were found in the neighborhood, and whenever a villager brought him items of value and beauty he endeavored to locate the source. For some time he was unsuccessful. It was not until he encountered an Arab villager who told him of a large mound near a remote village from which he and others had dug bricks for their own use that Botta hired two diggers and sent them to the spot with instructions to see what they could uncover. A week later an excited messenger reported that the diggers had unearthed ancient walls decorated with colored pictures, reliefs, carved images and drawings of extraordinary animals. Botta, hastening to the spot, was soon convinced that they had chanced upon the remains of an ancient and splendid palace, one perhaps erected by the Assyrians.

The ruins were on the east bank of the Tigris River about twelve miles north of Mosul, at a place called Khorsabad. It was later proved to be the ancient city of Dur Sharrukin. The walls were covered with sculptured alabaster slabs picturing battles, sieges, processions, hunting scenes and details of palace life; the walls extended over many acres.

At that time no one was able to read the cuneiform inscriptions, but later, when the secrets of the cuneiform were deciphered, it was found that this enormous palace, covering twenty-five acres, had been erected by Sargon II, who reigned 722–705 B.C. King Sargon had been so completely forgotten that the sole remaining reference to him was to be found in Isaiah 20:1, yet the palace was obviously one of the grandest in all history, housing one of the most glorious of emperors. When the news of this discovery reached Europe, the sensation it caused was enormous. It was much like that resulting from the return of Columbus with his report of the discovery of a new world, for to the people of Europe, and of France in particular, this was indeed the discovery of a new and forgotten world. Whereas previously the Nile Valley had been supposed to be the cradle of civilization, now this honor was given to the valley of the Tigris and Euphrates. The French government promptly appropriated generous funds to carry on the explorations; eventually Botta was able to publish five large volumes, with over four hundred pictures, describing his discoveries. From these pictures the people of Europe became familiar with the dress, armor, household implements and hunting methods of the ancient Assyrians whose great nation had thus suddenly been returned to the pages of history.

The next great name in the history of Biblical archeology is that of Sir Austen Henry Layard, an Englishman of French Huguenot descent. Fired by Botta's surprising discoveries, but with almost no financial backing, he went out to Mesopotamia to see what he could

SARGON II AND HIS VIZIER

Sargon reigned 722-705 B.C. and erected a palace covering
twenty-five acres.

find. He was fascinated by the large mounds that dot the region and, having secured a small financial gift, began to dig in Nimrud for the ancient city of Calah, some twenty miles southeast of Mosul and a mile and a half east of the Tigris River. Here he was incredibly successful. Within twenty-four hours he had uncovered portions of two magnificent Assyrian palaces. Everywhere he dug he uncovered rooms lined with alabaster slabs seven feet high covered with wonderful carvings and pictures. In Genesis 10:8–9 is the earliest known reference to Nimrud: "And Cush begat Nimrod: he began to be a mighty one in the earth. He was a mighty hunter before the Lord: wherefore it is said, Even as Nimrod the mighty hunter before the Lord." It was to this mighty hunter that local tradition had attributed the establishment of the city.

Speedily the story of Layard's success aroused the greed of the local Turkish governor, who determined to stop Layard's work unless he was given a share in the riches he thought were being uncovered. The pasha, or governor, sent his men at night to set up gravestones on the top of the mound and the next day ordered Layard's workmen to stop, claiming a cemetery was being desecrated. The work came to a standstill for a time, but fortunately the other oppressions and cruelties of the pasha aroused such hostility that he was removed from office. Soon Layard's excavations were allowed to proceed. One day shortly after, a great shout was raised and the diggers came toward Layard shouting and dancing, saying that they had found Nimrud himself. The object proved to be an enormous winged lion made of alabaster. It was later identified as an image of one of the Assyrians' four astral gods. Eventually an amazing collection of giant winged bulls with human heads and other deities with eagle heads was uncovered. A great number of these were shipped to the museums of England.

As the diggings progressed, fresh meaning was seen in Ezekiel's vivid description of that land (Chapter 31:3–12). "Behold the Assyrian . . . and all the people of the earth are gone down from his shadow, and have left him." And the scholars realized how completely the dire prophecy of Zephaniah had been fulfilled: "And he will stretch out his hand against the north, and destroy Assyria . . . every one that passeth by her shall hiss and wag his hand." (Zephaniah 2:13–15). The city was the city of Calah, mentioned in Genesis 10:11; the main palace was built by Ashurnasirpal II, who reigned c. 885–859 B.C.

KHORSABAD, VIEW FROM THE EAST

In 1849 Layard began digging a new site at Kuyunjik (or old Nineveh) on the banks of the Tigris opposite Mosul. In about four weeks of digging he uncovered the palace of Sennacherib, who reigned 704–681 B.C., and whose siege of Jerusalem is vividly described in II Kings, chapters 18 and 19. Many inscriptions were uncovered, and splendid walls built of glazed brick and lovely mosaics with white cuneiform lettering on a background of turquoise blue. Ordinarily the colors favored were black, yellow and dark blue. Some of the pictures reveal a high degree of artistic ability; one of the most famed is the depiction of a dying lioness. The city of Nineveh, surrounded by double brick walls, had been the capital of Assyria for only ninety years, but it had made itself a vast and powerful city. The inner walls were some thirty-two feet thick and seventy-six feet high, and there were fifteen towering gates and an outer moat some seventy-seven feet wide. A truly magnificent city.

Splendid as was the discovery of the palace of Sennacherib, "the like of which had never been seen," still more significant for the new science of archeology was the finding of two rooms in which were stored an amazing library, added to the palace by Sennacherib's grandson, Ashurbanipal. The books—or better, tablets—were found to have been arranged according to a definite system and included works on such subjects as exorcism, philosophy, astronomy, mathematics, philology, history, education, poetry and devotional music. They combined to present an astonishing summary of the knowledge of that era. At the time they were found no one could read them; their importance was only gradually realized. But the thrilling discovery of these old cities and palaces settled forever any question as to the glory of old Assyria. The actual deciphering of the inscriptions and tablets presented an intriguing challenge to the scholars of the day. For a time it was questioned whether these beautiful designs were writings; it was suggested that they might be purely ornamental. But through scholarly detective work the secret of the script was discovered. The man responsible for this remarkable achievement was Sir Henry Rawlinson, and the scene of his victory was Iran.

Henry Rawlinson, a cadet on board a ship sailing to India, had attracted the attention of an orientalist and statesman, the governor of Bombay, who was a passenger. Rawlinson's interest in Persian antiquities was aroused by this meeting, and when in later years he became a major in the British army and was assigned by the East India Company to Kermanshah as consul and representative in 1833, he found an opportunity to develop his knowledge of antiquity. His first concern was the problem of reading cuneiform writings, and he commenced with a study of the inscriptions at Ganj Nameh some six miles from Hamadan. He early decided that a certain combination of characters must stand for the word *king* and judged that the three persons referred to as kings in the inscription must be Darius, Xerxes and Vishtaspa. From this beginning he worked out the probable meaning of about one third of the syllabary. He then transferred his attention to the much larger and more complete inscriptions carved on the Besitun cliff about twenty-six miles from Kermanshah. Here the face of the cliff had been smoothed several hundred feet above the plain, and a series of figures in bas-relief had been carved, with very extensive cuneiform inscriptions beside and below the figures. From early times travelers had talked of

SLAB FROM THE PALACE OF ASHURNASIRBAL.
KING OF ASSYRIA   884-860 B.C.

RELIEF FROM PALACE OF ASHURNASIRPAL, KING OF ASSYRIA, 884-860 B.C.

these figures and tried to guess their meaning. One tenth-century traveler had thought the figures to be that of a schoolmaster and his pupils and thought the schoolmaster held in his hand a strap with which to beat the students. Another nineteenth-century traveler thought the carvings represented Jesus and the disciples, Judas being trampled underfoot, and the image of Ahuramazda representing the cross. Actually, as later investigation proved, the frieze shows King Darius facing his defeated enemies, who have been roped together, and one of whom he is treading underfoot, with the traditional figure of Ahuramazda at the top.

To copy this long inscription called for no little courage and persistence on the part of Rawlinson. Part could be copied by placing a ladder on a narrow ledge below the frieze. Part was copied by swinging down a ladder from above. Rawlinson was able to copy some 1,200 lines of carving in all. After laborious study he ascertained that three different languages were involved, and he succeeded in translating four hundred lines of the old Persian. He found the lines had been carved at the order of King Darius in 515 B.C. Darius describes how he seized the throne and defeated various rival pretenders. He tells the extent of his empire and calls down the curse of God on any who would destroy his work. The cuneiform was covered with a varnish that proved more durable than the stone itself and had preserved in a remarkable way this delicate writing for over 2,300 years.

Rawlinson published his translation of the Persian inscription in 1847. With the aid of other scholars in later years he translated and published the other two inscriptions, one in Elamite and one in Babylonian. The Babylonian tongue in particular proved amazingly complicated. The scholars found that a single sign might stand for a syllable or for a complete word and that the same sign might represent several different syllables or several different words; on the other hand, several different signs might express the same word. For a time there was seemingly hopeless confusion, until a tablet was found in Kuyunjik on which a list correlated the ideogrammatic script with the syllabic. Nearly a hundred of these tablets were found, comprising a nearly complete ancient dictionary.

So intricate were the problems involved and so difficult the translation of these ancient tablets, that there were many who scoffed and felt that the scholars were pretending to a knowledge they did

STATUE OF GUDEA, A KING OF SOUTHERN BABYLONIA. Note the
Cuneiform Inscription.

not possess. In order to test their accuracy, the British Museum determined on a searching trial. Making four copies of an inscription that had never been translated, museum authorities sent a copy to each of the four leading cuneiform scholars, asking them to translate it as speedily as possible and return it to the museum. One of these scholars was Rawlinson. Unknown to the others, each worked out his own translation and returned it to the museum. When the four translations were compared, they were found to agree in all important particulars, and the scholars were vindicated. Because of its importance in solving the problem of the old cuneiform, Besitun has been called the most important spot in Asia from the standpoint of archeology. And as a result King Darius, who is mentioned in the book of Ezra 5:5, 6:1–7, and in Haggai 1:1, and Zechariah 1:1, emerges as a living figure who had indeed ruled a mighty Persian empire as the Bible reveals.

It is not surprising that after the great excitement caused by these first discoveries and the acquisition of so many carvings and inscriptions, there was little additional investigation for some time. Thousands of tablets had been unearthed and brought to the museums of Europe, but there were few who could read them. The work of translation proceeded very slowly; with so many tablets unread there was little incentive to go out and find more.

After some years the British Museum employed a brilliant young scholar, the Assyriologist George Smith, to sort and classify their cuneiform tablets. As he was engaged in this work Smith found a curious tablet which had originally contained six columns but from which three had broken off. He discovered that it was the story of a ship resting on the top of a mountain named Nisir (Nizir). There followed an account of the sending forth of a dove which, finding no place to set its foot, returned to the ship. Suddenly Smith realized that he was reading a Chaldean account of Noah's flood. Such was his excitement that he fainted dead away! A London newspaper offered to finance an expedition to Mesopotamia to see whether Smith might find other evidence substantiating the story of the flood. In 1872 Smith went to Nineveh and extended the excavations of his predecessors. His most valuable finds were 384 additional tablets from the great library that had been accumulated by King Ashurbanipal. There were some 30,000 tablets in all, most of them copies of still earlier documents from the library of Babylon.

The main object of Smith's expedition, the finding of additional fragments of the story of the deluge, was successfully achieved, and in addition he found a story of the creation and many tablets describing the details of the lives of the Assyrians. During subsequent years, as the work of translating Ashurbanipal's great library went forward, such a mass of detail regarding life in old Assyria was revealed that scholars feel they know more of the daily life and ideas of Assyria than they do of England as it was only one thousand years ago.

*Courtesy of the University of Pennsylvania; from Collections in
the University Museum, Philadelphia*

MORE CYLINDRICAL SEAL IMPRESSIONS, BABYLONIA

# 2

# THE NEW FINDS AND GENESIS

IT IS INTERESTING TO COMPARE THE CREATION STORIES OF BABYLONIA and Assyria with the account given in the first chapters of Genesis. The Babylonian story relates:

> When on high the heaven had not been named,
> Firm ground below had not been called by name,
> Naught but primordial Apsu, their begetter,
> [And] Mummu-Tiamat, she who bore them all,
> Their waters commingling as a single body;
>
> .    .    .    .    .    .    .    .    .    .    .    .
>
> Then it was that the gods were formed within them.
> Lahmu and Lahamu were brought forth, by name they were
>   called.
>
> .    .    .    .    .    .    .    .    .    .    .    .
>
> Anshar and Kishar were formed, surpassing the others.
>
> .    .    .    .    .    .    .    .    .    .    .    .
>
> Yea, Anshar's first-born, Anu, was his equal.*

In the second and fourth tablets the battle between Marduk, the champion of the gods, and Tiamat, the god of chaos, is described.

---

* James B. Pritchard, *Ancient Near Eastern Texts Relating to the Old Testament* (Princeton: Princeton University Press, 1950), pp. 60-61. Square brackets indicate restorations; parentheses indicate interpolations.

Marduk is victorious, apparently signifying the conquest of darkness by light. Marduk takes up the body of Tiamat:

> He split her like a shellfish into two parts:
> Half of her he set up and ceiled it as sky,
> Pulled down the bar and posted guards.
> He bade them to allow not her waters to escape.
>
> . . . . . . . . . . . .
>
> He constructed stations for the great gods,
> Fixing their astral likenesses as constellations.
> He determined the year by designating the zones:
> He set up three constellations for each of the twelve months.
>
> . . . . . . . . . . . .
>
> The Moon he caused to shine, the night [to him] entrusting.*

In comparing the two stories, the Babylonian and the Bible, we find many similarities and many striking differences.

Both accounts tell of a time when everything was waste and void.

In the Bible we read of how light dispelled darkness and order took the place of chaos. In the Babylonian account the god Marduk fights and kills Tiamat, the goddess of chaos.

In the Bible God makes the dry land to separate from the sea. In the Babylonian account Marduk creates dust and pours it out by the water.

In the Bible we read that God makes the sun, moon and stars to rule in the heavens. In the Babylonian epic Marduk makes the stars for stations for the gods.

In Genesis God creates the animals and creeping things, in the Babylonian account it is an assembly of gods who make the animals.

In Genesis God makes man of the dust of the earth. Marduk makes him of blood and bone.

From a religious standpoint the differences between the two accounts are significant. One might expect that the higher material civilization of Babylon, with its arts and sciences, would produce a higher religion. The reverse is the case. The Jews attribute creation to one God and Creator, the Babylonians to a group of gods. In the Bible we learn that the creation of the world by God was a series of deliberate actions for the welfare of mankind. In the Babylonian myths the world is made as a sort of by-product of a war be-

* *Ibid.*, p. 67.

tween the gods and is created from a leftover carcass. Genesis tells of how the Spirit of God hovered in care over the waters and calmed them; in Babylon they taught of a furious battle in which demons overcame the gods of chaos. The Genesis account reveals one supreme and holy God; in Babylon they taught of many gods, who were deceitful, evil and warring among themselves. In short, where the Babylonian account gives us a morally valueless legend, the Bible gives an account we recognize as simple and beautiful and of deep religious significance. Although archeology shows how small and insignificant was the role of the Jewish people in the politics of the ancient world, it confirms how unique was their religious insight and provides cause for belief that in the realm of religion they were indeed a chosen people.

In the books of the Old Testament we have a picture of mankind gradually falling away from a belief in one God into the worship of many gods. According to Scripture the prophets of Israel and Judah were not originators of a new belief, but were men who recalled the people to their original faith in one God Yahweh, sometimes successfully, sometimes without success. As a result of the influence of Darwin's theory of evolution, the tendency among scholars in recent years has been to reverse this process. Polytheism, a belief in many demons and gods, they tell us, was the earliest form of religion, and it was the ultimate achievement of the Old Testament prophets that they rose to a belief in one God and persuaded their people of its truth. It may be of interest to inquire if archeological discovery has any light to throw on changing opinion.

First of all, archeologists have demonstrated beyond any question that progress is not automatic and that there is decay and decline as well as growth and improvement. Repeatedly the archeologist's spade has brought to light the remnants of a once great and flourishing civilization, a civilization that declined and was so completely forgotten that men doubted it had ever existed. Indeed it seems almost a rule of civilization that the rise of material prosperity and power is accompanied by a decline in religion and morals. Iran, Greece, Rome and Israel all tell of early years when honor and honesty, purity and loyalty to high ideals were characteristic of their people, and also of later periods of greater wealth, higher development of the arts and sciences, and decay and decline in matters of morals and religion. In time, also, moral and spiritual

decline leads to national decay and weakness and usually to a disintegration of the empire and the disappearance of the nation. One
who contrasts the society of the tent dwellers of Iraq today with the
rediscovered glories of old civilizations buried around them can
readily see how transient is worldly dominion. It is a dangerous in-
ference to conclude that because monotheism is a higher form of
religion, it must therefore necessarily be a later development than
polytheism.

The late Dr. Stephen Herbert Langdon, professor of Assyriology
at Oxford University and considered one of the great authorities
on cuneiform literature, wrote a book on Semitic mythology in
which he reached the conclusion that monotheism was, in fact, the
earlier belief. He writes: "I may fail to carry conviction in conclud-
ing that both in the Semitic and Sumerian religions, monotheism
preceded polytheism and the belief in good and evil spirits. The
evidence and reasons for this conclusion, so contrary to accepted
and current views, have been set down with care and with the per-
ception of adverse criticism. It is, I trust, the conclusion of knowledge and not of audacious preconception. . . . All Semitic tribes appear to have started with a single tribal deity whom they regarded
as the divine creator of his people. In my opinion, the history of the
oldest religion of man is a rapid decline from monotheism to extreme polytheism and a widespread belief in evil spirits. It is, in a
very true sense, the history of the fall of man."

Another scholar, Sir Peter le Page Renouf, the translator of the
Egyptian Book of the Dead, observed: "It is therefore more than
5,000 years since in the valley of the Nile the hymn began to the
unity of God and the immortality of the soul. The belief in the
Unity of the Supreme God and his attributes as Creator and Law-
giver, these are the primitive notions encased like indestructible
diamonds in the midst of mythological superfectations accumulated in the centuries. . . . It is incontestably true that the sublimer
portions of the Egyptian religion are not comparatively late results
of a process of development of elimination from the grosser."

It was also the conclusion of another scholar, Professor Schmidt
of Vienna, in his book *The Origin and Growth of Religion,* that
archeological evidence drawn from all round the world shows
among primitive people a widespread early belief in one Supreme
Being and in a future life.

As Dr. Langdon foresaw, so revolutionary a concept and one so
at variance with scholarly theories, was bound to be carefully scru-

inized and criticized. Particularly have questions been raised as to the precise meaning of monotheism in this connection. For while it is agreed that almost everywhere there was a belief in a supreme God, it is not so clear that he was in fact the only God. Rather he appears to be the unique and most powerful God, the creator, but usually if not always, the ruler over lesser gods or spirits. Most scholars today feel that Langdon and Schmidt somewhat overstated their case and that their views are not fully substantiated.

At the same time it must be recognized that archeology can never be expected to settle the question of whether or not our earliest ancestors were monotheists. For many thousands of years before there were any records primitive peoples were worshiping and traditions were developing. Long before writing was invented there must have been many shifts in beliefs, many long-range developments; it is unreasonable to expect to gain certain information from records written long after. Even during Biblical times, as Albright and Wright have pointed out, monotheism was rather a practical assumption and basis for action than a speculative theology. Yahweh the God was the ruler of all gods, the One known by his mighty acts as a God of power. Yet there are many indications that the gods of other nations were considered to have some sort of existence, subject to the commands and authority of Yahweh. These gods were weak, under Yahweh's judgment, and to be ridiculed. Yet they did exist. But for all practical purposes the only God to whom the people had to relate their lives and the only One whose laws must be obeyed was the great Yahweh. It remained for the speculative Greeks, long after, to evolve a philosophy of monotheism. The monotheism of the Hebrews was pragmatic and practical.

Certainly archeological investigation does disprove the idea—popular in some circles—that monotheism was a late achievement of the prophets of the eighth and seventh centuries B.C. There seems every reason to accept the Biblical picture of a monotheism introduced by Moses struggling for persistence during the troubled times of the Judges and revived and vitalized by King David and King Solomon. Dr. Albright concluded that "the cosmic monotheism of Solomon's Temple makes Mosaic monotheism a *sine qua non* for the comprehension of early Israelite religious history, since there is no suggestion in any of our sources that a paramount spiritual leader had arisen between Moses and David."*

* W. F. Albright, *Archaeology and the Religion of Israel* (Baltimore: Johns Hopkins Press, 1942), p. 155.

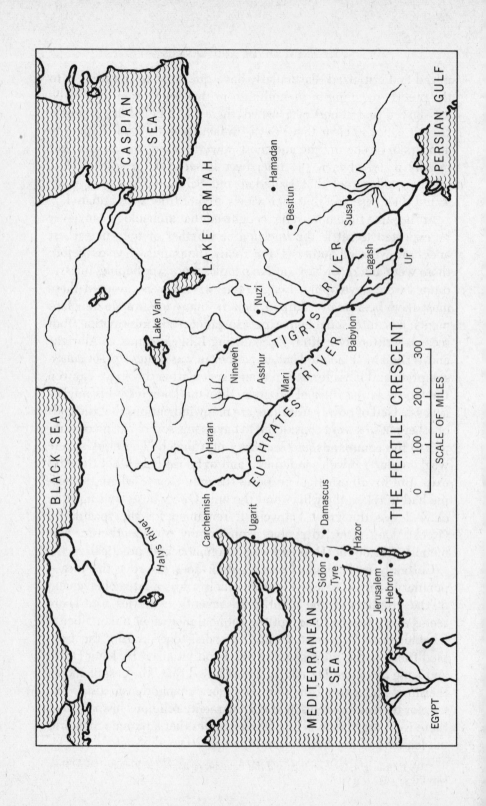

THE FERTILE CRESCENT

SCALE OF MILES

0    100    200    300

CASPIAN SEA

PERSIAN GULF

LAKE URMIAH

Hamadan

Besitun

Susa

Lagash

Ur

Nuzi

Babylon

TIGRIS RIVER

Lake Van

Nineveh

Asshur

Mari

EUPHRATES RIVER

Haran

BLACK SEA

Halys River

Carchemish

Ugarit

Damascus

Sidon

Tyre

Hazor

Jerusalem

Hebron

MEDITERRANEAN SEA

EGYPT

# 3

# THE FALL,
# THE PATRIARCHS
# AND THE FLOOD

IT IS NOT TO BE EXPECTED THAT THERE ARE ARCHEOLOGICAL REMAINS of the Garden of Eden mentioned in the second and third chapters of Genesis. But archeology has thrown light on the location the writer of Genesis had in mind in describing this traditional spot. In the second chapter of Genesis we read: "And a river went out of Eden to water the garden; and from thence it was parted, and became into four heads. The name of the first is Pison: that is it which compasseth the whole land of Havilah, where there is gold. . . . And the name of the second river is Gihon: the same is it that compasseth the whole land of Ethiopia. And the name of the third river is Hiddekel: that is it which goest toward the east of Assyria. And the fourth river is Euphrates."

There is no doubt about the last two. Hiddekel was a common name for what is today called the Dajjleh, or Tigris. But many guesses have been made as to the identity of the Pison and the Gihon. They have been identified with the Aras, the Nile, the Indus and other most unlikely choices. One quite possible identification for the Gihon is the Kerkha River in southwestern Iran; in times past, the Kerkha did flow with the Tigris and Euphrates into the Persian Gulf. However, Dr. Delitzsch found in Babylonia a list of the principal irrigation canals, among which were two names that seem to correspond with the names of these unknown streams. One was called the Pisanu which corresponds with Pison, and another was named Guhanu, obviously a variant spelling of Gihon. It is quite likely that these two canals, which were constructed at a

later date, are the boundaries of the old garden of Eden described
in this passage. Additional evidence for this supposition is that the
plain of Mesopotamia, to the south and west of old Babylon, is
referred to in early inscriptions as Edin, meaning "steppe desert."
Thus there is good reason to believe that this is the region indicated
in Genesis. At the same time it should be noted that Albright's conclusions, first published in 1922, identifying the Pison and Gihon
as the two Niles and placing the garden of Eden farther to the west,
is still favored by many.

In old Babylonian literature there are frequent references to a
Tree of Life, such as is mentioned in Genesis 2:9. Representations
of the tree are frequent in alabaster reliefs and seals. Its fruits were
supposed to confer eternal life on those who ate of them. One cyl-
inder seal impression among those found seems to be a depiction
of the temptation and the Tree of Life.

References to Noah's flood and long accounts of a deluge have
been found in both Babylonia and Assyria. The finest and most
beautiful poem to be discovered in ancient Babylonian literature is
the so-called Gilgamesh epic, containing two hundred and five
lines. The story is told of the great hero, Gilgamesh, visiting a per-
sonage named Ut-napishtim, who had become a god, and asking
him how it happened that this gift had been conferred upon him.
In reply he tells the story of the great deluge. Four of the gods, he
says, determined to destroy mankind. But Ea, the lord of the earth
whom Ut-napishtim worshiped, heard of the intention and warned
Ut-napishtim to prepare for the flood by building a boat for himself
and his family. Ut-napishtim built the ship, made it watertight with
pitch, stored it with food and drink and brought into it all kinds of
living creatures with his family, his workmen and a pilot. The sun
god Shamash fixed the time of the flood, as is vividly described:

> With the first glow of dawn,
> A black cloud rose up from the horizon.
> Inside it Adad thunders,
>
> . . . . . . . . . . . .
>
> Forth comes Ninurta and causes the dikes to follow.
> The Anunnaki lift up the torches,
> Setting the land ablaze with their glare.
> Consternation over Adad reaches to the heavens,
> Turning to blackness all that had been light.
>
> . . . . . . . . . . . .

The gods were frightened by the deluge,
And, shrinking back, they ascended to the heaven of Anu.
The gods cowered like dogs
    Crouched against the outer wall.

. . . . . . . . . . . . . .

Six days and [six] nights
Blows the flood wind,
As the south-storm sweeps the land.
When the seventh day arrived,
    The flood [-carrying] south-storm subsided in the battle,
Which it had fought like an army.
The sea grew quiet, the tempest was still, the floods ceased.
I looked at the weather: stillness had set in,
And all of mankind had returned to clay.
The landscape was as level as a flat roof.
I opened a hatch, and light fell upon my face.
Bowing low, I sat and wept,
Tears running down on my face.
I looked about for coast lines in the expanse of the sea:

. . . . . . . . . . . . .

On Mount Nisir the ship came to a halt.

. . . . . . . . . . . . .

When the seventh day arrived,
I sent forth and set free a dove.
The dove went forth, but came back;
There was no resting-place for it and she turned round.
Then I sent forth and set free a swallow.
The swallow went forth, but came back;

. . . . . . . . . . . . .

Then I sent forth and set free a raven.
The raven went forth and, seeing that the waters had diminished,
He eats, circles, caws, and turns not round.
Then I let out [all] to the four winds
    And offered a sacrifice.
I poured out a libation on the top of the mountain.
Seven and seven cult-vessels I set up,
Upon their plate-stands I heaped cane, cedarwood, and myrtle.
The gods smelled the savor,
The gods smelled the sweet savor,
The gods crowded like flies about the sacrificer.*

* Pritchard, *op. cit.*, pp. 94-95.

The following similarities between Genesis and the Babylonian story may be noted: The deluge is divinely planned. The hero is warned of the impending deluge. He builds a ship. It is made watertight with pitch. He brings aboard the animals. The storm comes and destroys all not on the ship. The storm ceases and the ship lands on a mountain top. The hero sends out birds; the last bird sent does not return. The hero makes a sacrifice on landing. The gods accept the sacrifice. He is given assurance for the future.

Nevertheless, there is a world of difference between the religious teachings of the two stories. In Genesis the flood is sent as a punishment of sin, to wipe out evil men. In the Babylonian story it happens as the senseless caprice of the gods. In Genesis Noah is saved because he is a righteous man and worthy. In the Babylonian story he is saved because he has a patron among the gods who warns him of the disaster to come. Genesis is monotheistic. The Babylonian story is the crudest of polytheism; the gods disagree, blame one another when things go wrong, cower like dogs before the flood, get hungry, swarm like flies to smell the sacrifice. One of the gods saves a man in order to anger the others; the one saved is given a place among the gods. Thus again the unique inspiration of the Biblical writer appears in the contrast between his interpretation of events and the legends current in the highest civilization of the day.

The recovery of copies of this epic at various places and in different languages reveals that traditional knowledge of a great, destructive flood was generally prevalent throughout Mesopotamia. At Larsa tablets bearing a list of former kings were found, giving the names of eight kings of fantastically long reigns, after which comes the notation: "The flood came. After the flood kingship was sent down from on high." There follow a list of "kings after the flood." Another ruler is mentioned as being one who loved to hear the stories of the "kings before the flood."

Some years ago Sir Leonard Woolley thought he had found direct evidence of the flood in his excavations at Ur. After digging through strata filled with the rubble and artifacts of an ancient city he came upon "perfectly clean clay, uniform throughout, the texture of which showed that it had been laid there by water."* After digging through eight feet of this clean clay, he again came upon layers of

---

* C. Leonard Woolley, *Ur of the Chaldees* (New York: Charles Scribner's Sons, 1930), p. 26.

rubble with stone implements and pieces of pottery of a different, earlier civilization. The conclusion seemed inescapable that he had uncovered evidence of an unprecedented flood which had put an end to one civilization. However, additional excavations in nearby places failed to prove that the flood layer was widespread, as he had asssumed it must be. What then is the explanation? There are various possibilities. Floods are notoriously capricious. Perhaps the same flood that had deposited silt in one spot had washed it away in another. Or perhaps the original "flood layer" which Woolley thought he had discovered was merely a sand bar thrown up by a minor flood. Again, the clean sand might have been wind-laid rather than water-laid during a long period of time when the site was unoccupied, although in such an event one might expect the sand layer to be general. But whatever the explanation it can no longer be considered certain that the English archeologist did indeed uncover a deposit left by Ut-napishtim's or Noah's flood.

The tendency among archeologists today is to believe that the flood stories point back to the enormous floods that must have accompanied the melting of the huge ice fields at the end of the last glacial era. Thanks to carbon-14 tests, it now appears that the last glacial epoch was much more recent than had been formerly supposed. Tests made on buried spruce wood and peat strata near Two Creeks, Wisconsin, show that the Wisconsin forests were overwhelmed about 9000 B.C. A thousand years later, Lake Huron and Lake Michigan were still half choked with glacial ice. This would bring the end of the last glacial period surprisingly close to the period of the earliest inhabited towns in the Near East. Radiocarbon tests on materials found at Jarmo in northern Iraq show that Jarmo was built up before 7000 B.C. The period of time between 8000 B.C., when the glaciers were retreating, and the founding of Jarmo was less than one thousand years. It is evident that the floods that must have marked the recession of the Ice Age would have been a comparatively recent memory. As Dr. Albright has pointed out, it is probably not accidental that there are no clear traditions of the Deluge in nearby Egypt, which must have escaped the worst of these floods.

# 4

# UR AND THE
# SUMERIANS

BEFORE ARCHEOLOGISTS BEGAN TO TURN UP THE SOIL OF MESOPOTA-
mia, Bible historians, knowing only that Abraham had lived in the
city of Ur, had no idea what sort of place it was or how advanced
the civilization. The region is a barren and forbidding desert today.
But thanks to the work of Sir Leonard Woolley and others, we know
how fertile a land it once was, and Ur has emerged as a once great
and wealthy city, the capital of a great nation. Originally, geologists tell us, the Persian Gulf extended as far north as the present
city of Baghdad. The Karun River flowed west into the gulf and
almost opposite it a now dried-up river flowed from Arabia. In the
course of time these two rivers filled the shallow Persian Gulf and
sealed it off with a great delta. North was a great lagoon, traces of
which still remain, which slowly filled with silt brought down by
the Tigris and Euphrates rivers. The new soil was light, deep and
rich, entirely free from stones, and because of the warm climate,
capable of producing three or four crops a year. Into this new and
fertile plain a race of people known as the Sumerians migrated. It
is not certain whence they came. Physically they were similar to the
types of people found in Afghanistan, Baluchistan and the Indus
Valley. Their rectangular seals strongly resemble those found along
the Indus River, and their civilization is similar to that of northwest
India in its terra cotta figures, its buildings and its art. It seems
probable that these early settlers came from southern Iran and
northern India, moving, perhaps, by water. This land became
known as Sumer and the northern portion of the great valley as

44

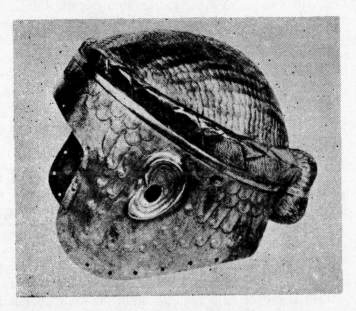

Meskelemdug's Helmet, found in the royal cemetery at Ur

Akkad. (Recent excavations point to the conclusion that lower Mesopotamia is slowly sinking; the lower levels of habitation are found to be at sea level and even lower. It may be that civilization in the region of Ur is much older than once seemed possible.)

Sumerian civilization was certainly one of the greatest of antiquity. It reached its height in the period of 2700–2400 B.C. The Sumerians in their architecture commonly made use of columns, arches, the vault and the dome—forms of building that made their way into Europe only thousands of years later. In arts and crafts they utilized gold and silver, not alone as ornamentation. Even household vessels, weapons and tools were made of precious metals. Copper was used, and there were, as well, many utensils of glass 'and stone—cups, vases and bowls of obsidian and lapis lazuli, the sapphire of the ancients.

The grave of an early prince named Meskelemdug, found in the royal cemetery at Ur, yielded some outstanding works of art. One of these was a helmet of beaten gold shaped like a wig, with fine lines showing the hair and a twisted engraved band about it. The ears, cheeks and head were protected and imitated in the shaping. In the grave were found bowls, a golden shell-shaped lamp inscribed with the prince's name, a golden dagger with a gold-studded hilt and a silver belt. There were two axes of electrum, hundreds of beads of gold and lapis lazuli and a quantity of jewels. In other places engraved shell plaques have been found, indicating remarkable artistry and draftsmanship. Their skill with these materials is all the more impressive when we recall that this was an agricultural region and raw materials were imported—bitumen from the north, copper from Oman, silver from Cilicia, gold from Elam and Antioch, diorite from the Persian Gulf and alabaster from Iran.

Although the Sumerians were skilled in the arts, the records they have left us reveal a cruel and ruthless civilization. The burial of certain great men, apparently kings or princes, was accompanied by human sacrifice on a lavish scale. The burial pits were crowded with the bodies of men and women apparently executed on the spot. In one grave, a guard of soldiers in copper helmets and armed with spears lay at the entrance. Nine ladies of the court, with elaborate golden headdresses, lay at the end of the tomb chamber. In front of the entrance were two heavy, four-wheeled carts, each drawn by three bullocks; the bones of the grooms and drivers lay nearby. In the grave of Lady Shub-ad court ladies lay in two parallel rows before her, with a harpist and a harp at the end of her bier, accompanied by two crouching servants. One can imagine with what terror the intimates of a king or queen watched the approach of the ruler's death, wondering which of them would be obliged to accompany the deceased to the other world.

In warfare the early Sumerians were completely merciless. Most of the prisoners taken in warfare were slaughtered at once and the survivors were held as lifelong slaves. Captured towns were not only looted but leveled and the surviving fugitives scattered abroad. There seems no doubt that one of the reasons for the ultimate dissolution of the Sumerian civilization was the practice of cruel and ruthless warfare.

In religion the Sumerians were, at the height of their empire, extreme polytheists. In many houses small figures of idols have been found, and these are doubtless of the type described as being taken by Rachel when she fled from her home with Jacob, in Genesis 31:27-32. The priests of these idols were many and greedy. Decrees issued by Urukagina, a reforming king of Lagash, directed

HEADDRESS OF LADY SHUB-AD

Note her four gold diadems and other gold jewelry. The head was copied
from a Sumerian statuette in the Louvre.

that high priests could no longer enter the garden of a poor woman and take wood or fruit from it. Urukagina ordered burial fees cut to a fifth of what the priests were charging and forbade the priests to claim the temple lands as their private possession.

At the same time their temples were centers of Sumerian education, with schools for scribes attached to most if not all of them. The writing of cuneiform with its hundreds of signs was a difficult art. And the amount of correspondence carried on was large, with practically all business transactions recorded. Many writing tablets have been unearthed; one side is written by the pupil and the other by the teacher. On some of the tablets the teacher had inscribed a list of signs with their phonetic value, syllables and symbols standing for ideas which the pupil reproduced on the other side. More advanced lessons showed paradigms of verbs and the declension of nouns. Mathematical tablets have tables showing how to extract the square root or the cube root and give formulae for calculation of the area of an irregular piece of land. It is hard for us to visualize Abraham struggling to extract the cube roots of large numbers, but possibly he did. Today the nomadic tribal chieftains whose flocks range western Iran and eastern Iraq often send their sons as far away as England for their education. May not Terah have sent Abraham to school under the priests of Ur? In the temples lists of weights and measures have been found, and Sumerian-Semitic dictionaries and tablets detailing medical knowledge such as primitive surgery, the values of herbs and magic formulae.

The outstanding religious edifice of Ur was the ziggurat, a sort of four-sided stepped pyramid built up in stages to an impressive height. It is thought that temples of this sort were built in imitation of mountain shrines honored in the lands from which the Sumerians had come. They had their practical use also as a refuge in time of flood. The ziggurat at Ur had a base two hundred by one hundred and fifty feet and was about seventy-five feet high. It was made of solid brick, the exterior of burnt brick and the remainder of mud brick. The upper terraces were irregular and probably once had trees growing on them. A flight of one hundred steps led to the top. The temple staff included priests, ministers of the harem, a minister of war, a minister of agriculture, a minister of transport and a minister of finance. Gifts brought for the gods were kept in huge storerooms. Receipts have been found for cattle, sheep, sacks of barley, cheese, butterfat and wool. In the enclosures were fac-

*Courtesy of the University of Pennsylvania*

TEMPLE OF ENLIL AT NIPPUR

tories where raw wool was spun. The weight of wool and the length
of cloth woven therefrom was carefully recorded. Profit and loss was
estimated in parallel columns.

In Abraham's time the city of Ur was about four by one and one-
half miles in extent. The streets were narrow and unpaved and
there was no vehicular traffic inside the city. Burdens were carried
by porters or animals. Most of the houses had two stories and twelve
to fourteen rooms.

All of these discoveries compel us to revise our view of Abraham's
place in history. We formerly thought of Abraham as a primitive
patriarchal figure standing at the very dawn of history. It is startling
to realize that he was the heir of a great civilization which had
reached its zenith nearly eight hundred years before his time.
Everywhere in Mesopotamia he would see thriving cities and
storied ruins.

Ur is a splendid example of the civilization of Abraham's day, but it is not absolutely certain that it was the city of his origin. For the Septuagint manuscripts omit the word *Ur* in this connection and, as we shall see, archeological evidence for the belief that his life was spent in the area around Haran is much stronger and more satisfactory. Apart from a single reference in Genesis 11:28 and 31, Abraham is always spoken of as a native of Haran.

It is not to be expected that the histories which kings of those times have left will contain mention of such a man as Abraham. But a tablet found in Babylonia bears the name Abarama and records that he paid his rent. At the least it shows that Abraham was one of the names used in that period. We next hear of Abram as living on the upper Euphrates River at a place called Haran, of which it is written "They settled there" (Genesis 11:31), and it is at Haran that Terah his father died. Excavations at a place called Mari have in recent years uncovered one of the most splendid palaces of all time, erected by King Zimri-Lim. The palace contains nearly three hundred rooms and covers over fifteen acres of ground. Archives were discovered containing over twenty thousand clay tablets, tablets which have suddenly thrown into sharp relief this old kingdom and reveal many links with Biblical history. For one thing, a surprising number of the names found in Genesis 11 have come to light as place names in the old Mari kingdom. Abram's brother was Haran, and the city of Haran is now shown to have been a flourishing city in the nineteenth and eighteenth centuries B.C. Another brother was Nahor, and the city of Nahor is frequently referred to in both Mari and Assyrian texts. Abram's father was Terah, and a city called Til-Turakhi is mentioned. The grandfather was Serug, the name of a town west of Haran. More remote is the name Peleg which corresponds with a town named Phaliga, then located on the Euphrates. The correspondence between these tribal or clan names and the names of cities then in existence is striking and complete.

Another store of tablets has been uncovered southeast of Nineveh in a city called Nuzi, and these have strikingly illuminated certain patriarchal customs alluded to in Genesis. Previous to their discovery it was perplexing to read Abram's prayer of complaint to God: "I continue childless, and the heir of my house is Eliezer of Damascus." Why should an outsider be his heir? In the Nuzi documents we find the answer. It was the custom for childless couples to adopt

*Courtesy of the Oriental Institute, University of Chicago*

ANCIENT NUZI CUNEIFORM TABLET, SHOWING A LIST OF PERSONAL
NAMES

someone whose duty it was to care for them while living and inherit their estate when they died. Apparently Eliezer was just such an adopted heir. However, if subsequently a son was born this arrangement was, in part, invalidated. In the cases of Sarah, Abram's wife, and Rachel, Jacob's wife, we read of their proposing to their husbands that they take handmaidens to provide the children the wives could not. This too is shown to be a custom of the time. Also, the last words of a dying man were accepted as a legal will and testament, as in Genesis 49 the dying Jacob designated Judah as the head of the family.

The Nuzi tablets also reveal that the family gods, called *teraphim* in Genesis, were considered of the highest importance, assuring the possessor of prosperity and guaranteeing the right of inheritance. From this we can understand Laban's anger and concern when he discovered that Jacob had disappeared and his teraphim with him, and his protest, "Wherefore hast thou stolen my gods?" It is because Jacob recognizes the righteousness of his father-in-law's indignation that he promptly promises, "Any one with whom you find your gods shall not live."

Following Abraham on his long trek, we pass to Dothan, Bethel, and Shechem, cities which archeology has shown to have been in existence in Abram's day. Furthermore, the Bible refers to the area south of the Dead Sea as being populous, with many flourishing cities, whereas the region today is barren, unproductive and almost uninhabited. But here also the spade of the archeologist has confirmed the accuracy of the picture given in Genesis. Dr. Albright of Johns Hopkins University has this to say: "The results of this and other numerous expeditions have definitely established the correctness of the very early Bible traditions that the Jordan valley was prosperous and densely populated when Abraham came into the country." The most prosperous period of history for the Jordan Valley was in the early Bronze Age (2500–2000 B.C.). Thereafter, the civilization declined and was never restored.

A recent article reports on the guidance modern colonists in Palestine have received from the Book of Genesis. A geologist, Xiel Federman, on the basis of Genesis 19:24 and 28, decided that natural gas and oil could be found in the Dead Sea area. Other geologists followed his lead and discovered geological evidence which convinces them that this is the case. Similarly, mention in Genesis of tamarisk trees growing in this region has induced colonists to try reforestation, with complete success. The cities of Sodom and Gomorrah have not been found, but traces of volcanic sulphur and lava rock bear witness to an early cataclysm similar to that described in the Bible. The water in the Dead Sea is slowly rising and submerged forests can be seen beneath its waters. It seems probable that Sodom and Gomorrah were on the submerged lowlands south of the Dead Sea. All in all, the description of this area around 2000 B.C., as given by archeologists, corresponds with remarkable fidelity to the region described in Genesis as it existed in the time of Abraham.

# 5

# JOSEPH AND THE EXODUS FROM EGYPT

THE STORY OF JOSEPH IS ONE OF THE MOST INTERESTING RELATED IN the Bible, telling as it does of one disgraced, sold into slavery, unjustly condemned, and rising to become the second in power in all the land of Egypt. The story is told with embellishments in the Koran, and it has been called the greatest short story ever written. A great many inscriptions have been found in Egypt but, to date, none that refers to Joseph and tells his story.

A few years ago, the tomb of a man named El Kab, governor of one of the provinces of Egypt and a contemporary of Joseph, was unearthed. An inscription on his tomb describes a terrible famine during the years of his rule and how the governor distributed to the famine sufferers the wheat he had stored during years of plenty. These events seem to have occurred during the years of the Hyksos kings and in many details the account parallels the method Joseph used to avert famine in the Genesis story. Furthermore, it should be noted that whereas in older days the land of Egypt was largely owned by small farmers, after the Hyksos reign nearly all the lands and fields of Egypt, excepting those belonging to the temples, were in the hands of the kings. Genesis 47:18–22 relates that when money was lacking the people of Egypt turned their lands over to pharaoh in exchange for food.

It is evident that the writer of the Biblical story of Genesis was well acquainted with Egyptian life and language. The titles "chief of butlers" and "chief of bakers" are mentioned in Egyptian inscriptions. The term "overseer of the house" is a translation of an

Egyptian title, as is "superintendent of granaries." Dreams were regarded as extremely important by the Egyptians, and the whole story of the rise of Joseph hinges on the interpretation of prophetic dreams. Pharaoh's birthday was always a time of feasting and rejoicing; that he should celebrate the occasion by the release of prisoners is certainly plausible. Magicians were plentiful at court and shepherds were held in abomination. The traditional length of a happy and prosperous life was one hundred and ten years (Joseph is said to have lived that long), and the mummification of great men a common custom.

In the last verses of Genesis it is told how Joseph adjured his relatives to take his bones back to Canaan whenever God should restore them to their original home, and in Joshua 24:32 it is told how his body was indeed brought to Palestine and buried at Shechem. For centuries there was a tomb at Shechem reverenced as the tomb of Joseph. A few years ago the tomb was opened. It was found to contain a body mummified according to the Egyptian custom, and in the tomb, among other things, was a sword of the kind worn by Egyptian officials.

The subsequent history of the Jewish people, their deliverance from Egypt, followed by the miraculous care of God during the forty years in the wilderness, and the conquest of Canaan, is borne out by the discoveries of archeologists, although the dates of these events are still obscure. In Psalm 105:26–43, God is praised for the great deliverance, and in the prophecies of Hosea, God's intervention is referred to repeatedly (Hosea 11:1; 12:9, 13; 13:4). It was then that the Hebrews became aware of Yahweh's choice of them as His people, it was then that they received His commandments, through Moses, and it was then that His wonderful interventions to save them revealed His power and might. A great deal of evidence supports the conclusion that there was a conquest of Canaan in the second millenium B.C. The difficulty is that some of the evidence points clearly to a date of about 1400, while other considerations would cause the conquest to be dated around 1250 B.C.

In favor of the older date is the chronology of the Bible. In I Kings 6:1, it is written that the beginning of the building of the temple occurred in the four hundred and eightieth year after the Exodus. Solomon ascended the throne about 965 B.C.; the temple was begun in the fourth year of his reign, or about 962; this would place the Exodus at 1442 B.C. and would make Thutmose III, who died in

BRICKMAKERS IN EGYPT

1441 B.C., the pharaoh of the Exodus. It is known from Egyptian records that Thutmose III was a great builder. An interesting tablet from his day has been found in which Semitic captives are pictured at work building him a temple. The "king who knew not Joseph" would then be this pharaoh Thutmose III, who ruled from 1495–1441 B.C. The establishment of a new dynasty would be likely to bring in a new set of favorites and cause the neglect of the old. If the Exodus was in 1442 and the Israelites spent forty years in the wilderness, they would have invaded Palestine around the year 1400.

Strong confirmation for this early date was found in 1888 when an Egyptian peasant woman stumbled on a collection of cuneiform tablets at a place called Tell el-Amarna. Altogether some four hundred tablets were found, written by various rulers in Palestine to the pharaoh in Egypt, and containing many references to incursions

by a people called the 'Apiru. One of the writers was Abdi-Hiba,
king of Jerusalem, who was greatly alarmed and implored the
pharaoh to send succor. "The 'Apiru plunder all the lands of the
king. If there are archers [here] in this year, the lands of the king,
my lord will remain [intact]; but if there are no archers [here] the
lands of the king, my lord, will be lost!" "The arm of the mighty
king conquers the land of Naharaim and the land of Cush but now
the 'Apiru capture the cities of the king. There is not a single governor [remaining] to the king, my lord—all have perished! . . . Behold Zimreda, the townsmen of Lachish have smitten him, slaves
who have become 'Apiru."*

The letters have given rise to lively discussion as to just who the
'Apiru may have been. Certainly the resemblance between *Apiru*
and *Hebrew* is striking; there seems little doubt that there is some
relationship between them. Some historians consider that the term
'Apiru was used to signify lawless and rebellious elements, much as
the term "bandits" is used today to denote opponents of certain governments. But whatever may be the exact significance, the letters
clearly reveal that strong, hostile elements were moving against the
constituted authorities of Palestine and threatening Egyptian rule.
In other letters from the king of Canaan, the pharaoh is besought
to send troops against the Sa Gaz, barbarians from the desert, who
are identified as being the 'Apiru.

In addition, there has been some evidence from excavations of
destructive invasions of certain cities in Palestine around the year
1400. Dr. John Garstang of the University of Liverpool was convinced that one of the city layers at Jericho represented a walled
city destroyed or burned about that time. There is much evidence
of a great conflagration, and Garstang and his associates collected
nearly a hundred thousand pieces of pottery from the ruins. Nearby, to the northwest, they found a cemetery containing quantities
of unbroken pots matching the potsherds found in the city. These
graves have been dated by means of some eighty Egyptian scarabs,
including scarabs from the early eighteenth dynasty, Hatshepsut,
Thutmose III and Amenhotep III, who reigned 1413–1377 B.C.
There were none later than 1400.

Garstang's conclusion regarding the city of Ai was that it had
been destroyed around the middle of the Bronze Age, about 1400

* Pritchard, *op. cit.*, pp. 488-489.

B.C. Later excavations at Jericho have led some to believe that its destruction came much earlier than supposed, and the destruction of Ai is now put at about 2200 B.C.

Most indications, however, point to a later date for the Exodus. One of these is the uncovering of the store-city of Pi-tum in the land of Goshen. In Exodus 1:11 it is written that the Israelites were compelled to work on the construction of Pi-tum and of Ramses, both designated as treasure cities. The archeologist Edouard Naville discovered that Pi-tum was indeed a store-city, with treasure chambers strongly built and separated by eight-foot brick walls. Some of the sun-baked bricks were molded with straw and some without, suggesting the refusal of the taskmasters to give the Israelites straw for the brickmaking, as told in Exodus 5:7. Almost the entire area of the city was occupied by these treasure rooms. According to inscriptions, the city was built by Ramses, who reigned about two hundred years after Thutmose III. It is also a matter of record that most of the construction work done under Thutmose III was done in the south, in upper Egypt. It is, of course, possible that these cities were begun by the Hebrews, abandoned when they fled from Egypt and later completed by Ramses, who ruled 1290–1224 B.C.

Another strong argument for a later date is that a large number of archeological surveys in Edom, Moab and Ammon have consistently shown that these kingdoms were not founded until the thirteenth century B.C. But the Book of Joshua describes these kingdoms as flourishing in Joshua's time. It seems likely that the conquest of Canaan was not achieved in a short time. Indeed, the Book of Joshua makes this clear. But as yet it has not been possible to satisfactorily harmonize all the data. If Ramses II was the pharaoh of the Exodus, then the children of Israel may have worked for him some ten years, fled the country about 1290 B.C., reached Palestine forty years later and began the conquest in 1250. If their stay in Egypt is added to this, it would mean they had first entered Egypt about 1720 B.C. This would then correspond with the time when the Hyksos dynasty first conquered Egypt in an invasion sweeping in from the north.

Merenptah, the son of Ramses II, left on record the first and only inscription so far found in Egypt which contains the name "Israel." It is on a large black granite stela which was found in Merenptah mortuary temple at Thebes. In about 1219 B.C. Merenptah caused

BRICKMAKING, A WALL PAINTING FROM THE TOMB OF

this record of his victories to be carved on the stela. The result, he
wrote, was that "The princes are prostrate, while they say 'Peace'.
There is no one who raises his head among the Nine Bows. Libya
is ruined, Khatti is pacified; the Canaanite land is despoiled with
every evil. Ascalon is carried captive, Gezer is conquered; Yano'am
is made as though it did not exist. The people Israel is desolate, it
has no offspring; Palestine [Khurv] has become a widow for Egypt.

*Courtesy of the Metropolitan Museum of Art*

REKH-MĬ-RE, VIZIER OF UPPER EGYPT, ABOUT 1450 B.C.

All lands are united, they are pacified."* From this it is evident that by 1219 B.C., the Israelites had become a recognized people. This would also seem to favor an earlier date for the Exodus. We shall return to this question in discussing the conquest of Canaan.

* Quoted in Jack Finegan, *Light from the Ancient Past* (Princeton: Princeton University Press, 1946), p. 105.

# 6

# MOSES AND CONTEMPORARY CODES

IT IS IMPOSSIBLE TODAY TO BE SURE OF THE EXACT ROUTE OF THE Israelites from Egypt, though the first stages of their journey can easily be identified. The groves and springs at which they rested are still there. The term translated as *Red Sea* means *reed sea*, and probably refers to an arm of the Red Sea, shallow and heavy with clumps of reeds which might be driven flat by a strong wind, as described in Exodus.

A surprising parallel to one of the miracles related in Exodus is told by Major C. S. Jarvis, a former British governor of Sinai. His desert camel corps camped near a spot where a small trickle of water coming from the limestone cliffs gave promise of finding a more adequate water supply. His men commenced to dig. A misdirected blow upon the limestone brought a piece of the face of the cliff crashing to the ground and a stream of clear, cold water came gushing from the porous rock in precisely the manner described in Exodus 17:6, when Moses struck the rocky cliff and water poured forth.

Perhaps the chief difficulty in believing the story of the Exodus as it has been written is the very large numbers of people said to have been involved. In the two census figures recorded in the Book of Numbers, the total number of men is given as being about six hundred thousand. Adding to this the probable number of women and children, the total would come to at least two million people, far more than could be sustained on that barren land or watered from the small fountains. Flinders Petrie has suggested that the word translated as *thousand* should be translated *family* or *tent*. Hence, when it is recorded that the Reubenites were comprised of 43,730, it should be translated as forty-three families, or seven hundred and thirty individuals. Some experts in Hebrew are unwilling to accept this interpretation of the word; but the Revised Version translated the word as *clan* in Micah 5:2 where the old version had *thousands*. It is evident that this possible meaning of the word, if used, would reduce the total number of Israelites at the time of the Exodus to between five and six thousand people, which is a much more reasonable and quite plausible figure. Another explanation sometimes given is that these figures may actually be those of King David's census, at a much later time when the kingdom had grown mightily, and mistakenly attributed to the time of Moses.

The Bible relates the manner in which God revealed His laws to Moses during the Israelites' stay in the wilderness. In the past many critics expressed the belief that these laws must have been of a much later date, excepting perhaps the Ten Commandments, because the Israelites were not known to be able to write at that time; the laws are such as concern a later and more developed civilization. On this difference of opinion archeology has shed much light.

Perhaps the most important find bearing on the laws of Moses was made in Iran on the site of Shushan by the French archeologist Jacques de Morgan.* In the course of excavations in 1884 De Morgan uncovered extensive remains of a splendid palace dating from Persian times and thought to be identical with the one about which the story of Esther centers. Here he found a great quantity of archeological treasures so extensive that two complete rooms of the Louvre have been set apart to hold them. In 1900–1902 De Morgan led another expedition which uncovered the broken pieces of an ancient legal code, the code of King Hammurabi of Babylon. Hammurabi was formerly thought to have reigned about 2000 B.C., but recent excavations at Mari on the Euphrates have almost positively established his reign as 1728–1676 B.C. Many inscriptions name Hammurabi as the great ruler who unified Babylon and established the empire. His conquests extended to the Mediterranean Sea. Many letters reveal his amazingly efficient organizing ability. He rebuilt the city of Babylon with straight, broad streets. In one of

* For a full treatment of this subject, see pp. 182-195, in Ira M. Price, *The Monuments and the Old Testament* (Philadelphia: Judson Press, 1958).

his letters he speaks of the second year of his reign as that year in which he established justice; this he did by collecting and codifying the laws of the kingdom, most of them handed down from generation to generation, as far back as Sumerian times. The laws were set up in the temple of Marduk for all to see, beautifully carved on a diorite column about seven feet high and six feet in circumference at the base.

The code of Hammurabi contains two hundred and forty-seven laws, written in thirty-six hundred lines. The bas-relief figure at the top is that of Hammurabi standing before the god Shamash, patron of law and justice, from whom he is about to receive divine law and authority. Rays shining from the shoulders of Shamash reveal his glory. He extends to Hammurabi a ring and a staff, the emblems of royalty and power.

The prologue to the code states that the gods had called forth Hammurabi to make righteousness shine forth and to protect the poor and the oppressed. There follows a summary of the laws and customs of the day and a set of precedents for their enforcement. The first section deals with property matters under three headings, personal, trade and commerce. The second section contains laws dealing with the family, with injuries and with labor legislation. The similarity between the code of Hammurabi and the laws of Moses will be evident in a comparison of a few quotations from each.

Exodus 21:2. "If thou buy a Hebrew bondman, six years he shall serve: and in the seventh he shall go out free for nothing." Hammurabi 117. "If an obligation come due against a seignior and he sold (the services of) his wife, his son or his daughter, or he has been bound over to service, they shall work (in) the house of their purchaser or obligee for three years, with their freedom re-established in the fourth year."

Exodus 21:15. "He that smiteth his father or his mother shall surely be put to death." Hammurabi 195. "If a son has struck his father they shall cut off his hand."

Exodus 21:16. "And he that stealeth a man and selleth him, or if he be found in his hand, he shall surely be put to death." Hammurabi 14. "If a seignior has stolen the young son of a(nother) seignior, he shall be put to death."

Exodus 21:24. "Eye for eye, tooth for tooth, hand for hand, foot for foot." Hammurabi 196-97. "If a seignior has destroyed the eye

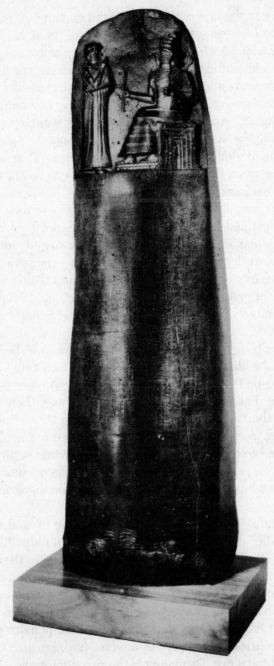

CODE OF HAMMURABI FOUND AT SUSA

of a member of the aristocracy, they shall destroy his eye. If he has broken a(nother) seignior's bone, they shall break his bone."

Exodus 21:26. "And if a man smite the eye of his servant, or the eye of his maid, and destroy it, he shall let him go free for the eye's sake." Hammurabi 199. "If he has destroyed the eye of a commoner or broken the bone of a commoner, he shall pay one mina of silver."

Exodus 21:28. "And if an ox gore a man or woman to death, the ox shall surely be stoned, and its flesh shall not be eaten, but the owner of the ox shall be quit." Hammurabi 250. "If an ox, when it was walking along the street, gored a seignior to death, that case is not subject to claim."

Exodus 21:29. "But if the ox was wont to gore in time past and it hath been testified to its owner, and he hath not kept it in, but it hath killed a man or a woman, the ox shall be stoned, and its owner shall be put to death." Hammurabi 251. "If a seignior's ox was a gorer and his city council make it known to him that it was a gorer, but he did not pad its horns (or) tie up his ox, and that ox gored to death a member of the aristocracy, he shall give one half mina of silver."

Exodus 22:1,4,3b. "If a man shall steal an ox, or a sheep, and kill it or sell it, he shall pay five oxen for an ox and four sheep for a sheep. If the theft be found in his hand alive, whether it be ox, ass, or sheep, he shall pay double. If he have nothing, then he shall be sold for his theft." Hammurabi 8. "If a seignior stole either an ox or a sheep or an ass or a pig or a goat, if it belonged to the church (or) if it belonged to the state, he shall make thirtyfold restitution; if it belonged to a private citizen, he shall make good tenfold. If the thief does not have sufficient to make restitution, he shall be put to death."

Exodus 22:2. "If the thief be found breaking in, and be smitten so that he die, there shall be no blood guiltiness for him." Hammurabi 21. "If a seignior make a breach in a house, they shall put him to death in front of that breach and wall him in."

In comparison with more humane laws today, Hammurabi's code seems very harsh and cruel. There are thirty-two crimes for which capital punishment is provided. Burning is the penalty prescribed for a temple priestess who opens a wine shop, for incest and for a looter caught at a fire. Drowning is the penalty for cheating in selling drinks, adultery, being a careless or reckless wife and for deserting a husband's home during his enforced absence. A woman

who had brought about the death of her husband is to be impaled
on a stake. Bodily mutilation is the penalty for many offenses; a
slanderer is branded, the slave who injures his owner's son is to lose
an ear, an eye is put out of one who destroys another's eye, the
hand of the surgeon who performs a fatal operation is cut off and
the tongue of a slanderous son is cut out.*

More fundamental is the fact that the code of Hammurabi and
other similar codes are essentially civil codes with but an intro-
ductory reference to a god; the laws of Moses are essentially religious laws and to be traced to the direct commands of God. Such
a detailed codification of laws existed in the Near East centuries
before the time of Moses. The critical view demanding a much
later date for the laws of Moses thus seems to be without support.

Another discovery of the highest significance was made at Ras
esh-Shamra in Syria in 1928. While plowing a field about ten miles
north of Latakia and half a mile from the coast a peasant woman
uncovered signs of an ancient building. Reports were sent to Beirut.
The following year excavations began under the direction of archeologists Claude Schaeffer and George Chenet. The ancient city
they uncovered proved to be Ugarit, founded before 2000 B.C. and
a flourishing center of commerce and culture in the fifteenth century B.C., the nearest port to the island of Cyprus and an important
crossroads of trade for the Near East.

The most important find was a library of what seems to have
been a school for priests and scribes in which there were hundreds
of cuneiform tablets in eight or nine different languages. The tablets mention the Hurrians, Hittites and the Hebrews. The city and
school were destroyed around 1400 B.C., or about the time when
the Tell el-Amarna letters record the encroachment of the 'Apiru.
The tablets are from an inch and a half to ten inches in height, include bilingual and trilingual lexicons and record commercial transactions, letters, exercises in grammar and religious poetry.

The examples of religious literature found at Ugarit reflect a belief in many gods, with one supreme god who is called El. El, of
course, is a name for God frequently used in the Old Testament, as
in Genesis 33:20, and in many place names such as Bethel (the
house of God) and Penu-el (the face of God). One of the Ugarit
tablets contains a picture of the god El enthroned and the king of
Ugarit in the act of making an offering.

* Pritchard, *op. cit.*, pp. 166-167.

HITTITE INSCRIPTIONS

Significant is the fact that many of the sacrifices mentioned in these tablets, from the time of Moses or earlier, use exactly the same terms as are used in the Old Testament. An offering without blemish, a holocaust, a trespass offering, a wave offering, a tribute offering and first fruits, are all denoted by terms similar to those mentioned in the Book of Leviticus. The seething of a kid in its mother's milk is a part of the ritual for producing rain—a rite forbidden in Exodus 23:19. There are many references to Baal, called the son of El and Asherah. Certain critics have said that the reference to Asherah in I Kings 18:19 could not be authentic because Asherah-worship came much later; it is now seen to have begun long before the composition of the Book of Kings. Reference is made to a man named Dan'el, a primordial hero who is said to "render justice to widows and orphans." It seems highly probable that this is the Daniel referred to in Ezekiel 14:14-20 rather than the compiler of the Book of Daniel, who was a contemporary of Ezekiel.

The finds at Ugarit, like the finding of Hammurabi's code and similar codes, have a direct bearing on the revision of the dates of the laws found in the Pentateuch. The Ras esh-Shamra tablets place the ritualistic legislation in an entirely new light. At one time it was generally held that the ritual laws and sacrifices described in the Pentateuch must have been evolved by a slow process in the centuries after the time of Moses. Now it appears that many were widely known and practiced before the time of Moses; a late date for the laws of the Pentateuch is no longer mandatory. This is not to deny the possibility that the laws of the Pentateuch as we now have them may include many additions and revisions made to fit changing conditions. Indeed, most critics believe that they do include such revisions. But it does show that many of them were far older than had been thought possible and so may well have come from Moses himself. In any case, it is evident that traditional rituals were adapted and made fit for use in worshiping the one true God. They were, in short, cleansed of polytheistic elements.

Just as the findings of the archeologists have brought new light on the laws of the Pentateuch, so they have brought the meaning of a covenant, and covenant relationship, into a new and sharper focus. The discovery of numerous international treaties drawn up in Asia during the second millenium B.C. has produced a wealth of close and illuminating parallels to the covenant relationship between Yahweh and Israel established in the time of Moses. Dr.

G. D. Mendenhall of the University of Michigan has made these parallels a subject for careful study. He points out that two sorts of treaties have been recovered: parity treaties, or treaties between two equal powers, and suzerainty treaties, in which a great protecting power concludes a treaty with a much weaker power. Only the treaties of the second class resemble the Covenant between God and Israel. Dr. Mendenhall defines a covenant as a promise or a bond undertaken between two legal communities when there is no other legal method of enforcement of its provisions, and distinguishes six elements in suzerainty treaties, all but one of which parallel the Old Testament relationship between Yahweh and Israel. They are as follows:

1. The Great King is identified in a preliminary phrase: "Thus says the Great King." Compare this with Exodus 20:1, where Yahweh identifies himself, saying: "I am the Lord thy God."

2. The benevolent deeds of the Great King are rehearsed in an historical survey. With this compare Exodus 20:1, "which have brought thee out of the land of Egypt, out of the house of bondage," and also Joshua 24:2–13, which gives a much more detailed summary of Yahweh's deeds, from the call of Abraham through the conquest of Canaan.

3. The obligations of the vassal are specified, prominent among them being a prohibition against his having foreign relations with other powers. So too the Covenant of Israel stresses the obligation to have no dealings with other gods (Exodus 20:3, 34:14, Joshua 24:14).

4. A stipulation that the text of the agreement must be deposited in the sanctuary of the vassal and read at intervals. So Moses gave the law into the keeping of the priests in charge of the ark of the Covenant and charged them to read it publicly every seven years. In Exodus 25:16 and 21 we read that it was placed in the ark of the Covenant.

5. A fifth section invokes various gods as witnesses of the covenant. Such a stipulation would be out of place in an agreement between the one true God and His people. However, in Joshua 24:22, the people are charged to become witnesses against themselves, and in later days the prophets call on heaven and earth to bear witness to the apostasy of Israel (Isaiah 1:2, Micah 6:2).

6. The agreement concludes with a list of blessings and curses that will come to those who keep or break the covenant. For paral-

lels, see Exodus 23:20–33, Leviticus 26:1–46 and Deuteronomy 27–28, where both blessings and curses are described in exhaustive detail.

The meaning of the term *covenant* and the significance of the covenant relationship between God and Israel have acquired a new importance in the minds of scholars. Dr. Albright concludes: "The concept of 'Covenant' dominates the entire religious life of Israel. . . . We cannot understand Israelite religion, political organization or the institution of the Prophets without recognizing the importance of the word 'Covenant.' "*

* W. F. Albright, *From the Stone Age to Christianity* (New York: Doubleday-Anchor Books, 1957), p. 16.

# 7

# THE CONQUEST
# OF CANAAN

## The Hittites, Period of the Judges

THE CITY OF JERICHO, WHOSE "WALLS CAME TUMBLING DOWN," IS A
site known and marked by a large mound about seventy feet high
and covering about sixty thousand square meters. Located near
an abundant flowing spring and serving as the door to Palestine,
Jericho has been occupied from the earliest times. Repeated excavations have been carried out during the past twenty-five years,
with somewhat baffling and contradictory results. The most recent
of these expeditions established that Jericho is one of the oldest
cities ever uncovered, its lowest level going back to about 6800 B.C.
and antedating the lowest level of the Tepe Gawra in upper Mesopotamia.

One would think that Dr. John Garstang's examination of the
ruins and his careful dating of the scarabs would be beyond challenge, but there are many today who consider the city he found
to be much older than originally estimated. How the scarabs of
fifteenth-century kings could be placed in graves of the twenty-
third century B.C. is not immediately evident. Certainly the ruins
Garstang uncovered correspond amazingly to the city described
in Joshua. He found the following correspondences with that city:
It was surrounded by double walls connected on the top by beams,
upon which houses had been built, as described in Joshua 2:15.
The walls had fallen down flat. The underlying layer of earth was
undisturbed; there was no evidence that the walls had been under-
mined. There was a single gateway to the city, as mentioned in
Joshua 2:5–7. The city had certainly been destroyed by fire, as the
thick layer of ashes and charred remnants of beams and pots at-

70

tested, and it is so reported in Joshua 6:24. The city had not been looted before it was burned, as one would expect. Wheat, lentils, onions, dates and dough were found in clay jars. Joshua strictly forbade all looting (Joshua 6:17–18). Lastly, no other city was built on the site for centuries, which accords with Joshua 6:26 and I Kings 16:34. In all these respects the Jericho destroyed somewhere around 1500 B.C. corresponds remarkably to the city and situation described in the Book of Jericho.

The Book of Joshua describes how Joshua defeated five Canaanite kings in the valley of Aijalon, passed by the fortress of Gezer (eventually captured by King Solomon) and took the fortress of Libnah at the head of the Elah Valley. Excavations at Libnah have shown that the fortress was occupied during the thirteenth century B.C. Next Joshua took the stronghold at Lachish where extensive excavations have been made. Digging revealed a whole series of cities, superimposed one atop another, beginning in the early Bronze Age. The ruins of a large temple were found, with quantities of bones of sheep, oxen and other animals obviously offered as sacrifice. Most of these bones were of the right foreleg. A law in the Book of Leviticus, 7:32–33, reads: "And the right shoulder shall ye give to the priest for an heave offering of the sacrifices of your peace offering. He among the sons of Aaron that offered the blood of the peace offerings and the fat, shall have the right shoulder for his part."

Also found at Lachish is a scarab of Pharaoh Amenhotep III, commemorating the killing with his own hands of more than one hundred lions during the first ten years of his reign.

For the purpose of dating the destruction of the fortress, the most important find was a broken bowl on which, in the Egyptian tongue, an inscription had been written by an Egyptian tax collector acknowledging the delivery of a wheat shipment in the fourth year of the reign of the pharaoh of Egypt. The writing resembles that ascribed to the reign of Merenptah. The fourth year of Merenptah's reign was 1220 B.C. Since the bowl was found among the ashes of the burned city, this would seem to date the destruction quite accurately. All the same, in one of the Tell el-Amarna letters, written after 1370 B.C. by Abdi-Hiba, king of Jerusalem, it is reported that Lachish had been plundered by the 'Apiru. So again we have the baffling question of which of two dates, two hundred years apart, is more nearly accurate in placing the destruction of Jericho by

THE WALLS

One of the oldest cities ever uncovered, Jericho was originally
is much archeological evidence to support the story

OF JERICHO

surrounded by double walls, with only a single gateway. There
of its destruction as related in the Book of Joshua.

Joshua. There is no doubt that Lachish was burned around 1225.
But was this the work of Joshua or of a later invader? Perhaps it was
Merenptah himself, who, as we have seen, boasted that "the people
of Israel is desolate. Palestine has become a widow." The earliest
mention we have of Aijalon is in the same Tell el-Amarna letters,
in which Abdi-Hiba reports that the 'Apiru are marching against
Aijalon and that one if his caravans has been plundered.

Joshua, passing on from Lachish, is reported to have captured
Heber and Debir. At Debir, later known as Kirjath-sepher, "the
city of scribes," a center of Canaanite culture, extensive excavations have uncovered the remains of an Israelite city, a beautiful
scarab from the time of Amenhotep III (1405–1370 B.C.) and a
great burned layer from the end of the Bronze Age, around 1200
B.C. The fact that the Israelite city is above the burned layer supports the later date for the conquest of Canaan.

In the latter part of the Book of Joshua we have a description of
an alliance of the tribes and kings of northern Palestine against
Joshua and his conquering host, an alliance which Joshua struck
and scattered by the waters of Lake Merom. It is written that following this Joshua turned on the city of Hazor, which "before time
was the head of all those kingdoms," killed all the inhabitants and
burned the city. Recently, for the first time, large-scale excavations
have been undertaken on the huge mound that represents this
ancient city. There are in fact two mounds about nine miles north
of the Sea of Galilee, both of unusual size. The city proper is represented by a hill nearly 2,000 feet long, 218 yards wide, and 43 yards
high; the fort, by a mound measuring 1,312 by 765 yards. This latter
was surrounded by massive walls 90 yards thick. It is estimated
that the fortress of Hazor could accommodate thirty thousand people in time of emergency.

We find many references to Hazor in secular and sacred history.
It is mentioned in an Egyptian execration list of the nineteenth
century B.C. as a potential enemy of the empire. Two letters found
in Mari, dated about 1700 B.C., refer to it. It is listed among the
cities captured by Thutmose III, by Amenhotep II and by Seti I.
Four of the Tell el-Amarna letters refer to Hazor, and it was the
city of Sisera, captain of the hosts of Jabin, king of Hazor. Solomon,
in I Kings 9:15, is reported to have rebuilt it, and Tiglath Pileser, in
II Kings 15:29, to have captured it. Clear evidence of this last event
was found in the ruins of a Hazor destroyed by fire in the second
half of the eighth century B.C. Many beautiful vases of basalt and

pottery were found intact, suggesting sudden evacuation of the
city, and flight. Preliminary excavations by Dr. John Garstang indicated that the fortress had been destroyed about 1400 B.C., a destruction which he identified with that by Joshua. Later excavations by the Rothschild expedition in 1955 uncovered a mass of
Mycenaean pottery of a typical thirteenth-century pattern, estab-
lishing the date of the destruction of the city as being around 1200
B.C. A find of special interest was a fragment on which were written
the two letters L T, meaning goddess, in a Proto-Sinaitic alphabet. The Rothschild dig strengthens the argument for a later date
for the conquest of Canaan.

## THE HITTITES

One of the striking confirmations of Bible history to come from
the science of archeology is the "recovery" of the Hittite peoples
and their empires. Here is a people whose name appears again and
again in the Old Testament, but who in secular history had been
completely forgotten and whose very existence was considered to
be extremely doubtful. In Genesis 23:10, it is told that Abraham
bought a parcel of land for a burying place from Ephron the
Hittite. In Genesis 26:34, Esau takes a Hittite girl for wife, to the
great grief of his mother. In the Book of Exodus, the Hittites are
frequently mentioned in the lists of people whose land the Hebrews
set out to conquer. In Joshua 11:1–9, the Hittites join in the confed-
eration of nations that try to resist Joshua's advance, only to be defeated by the waters of Merom. In Judges, intermarriage occurs between the Hebrews and the Hittites. In I Samuel 26, Hittites en-
roll in David's army, and during the reign of Solomon he makes
slaves of the Hittite element in his kingdom and allows his people
to take Hittite wives. But until the investigations of modern archeologists, the Hittites remained a shadowy and undefined people.

Clay tablets found in Assyria and Egypt give us our first picture
of the Hittites and their way of life. Egyptian artists depicted them
as having features we identify as Armenian, and it seems more than
likely that the Hittites were the ancestors of the Armenian race.
An Egyptian tablet records a fierce battle between Ramses II and
the Hittites at Kadesh on the Orontes River in 1287 B.C. On the
first day of battle Ramses was defeated and captured, but the timely
arrival of reinforcements on the second day turned the tide of
battle, rescued him from the Hittites and accomplished their com-

plete overthrow. So heavy were the losses that the Hittites killed their own leaders and fled to their homes.

It remained to Dr. A. H. Sayce, the Assyriologist, and Dr. William Wright, a missionary at Damascus, to recover the first actual remains of the Hittites. In time these were found throughout western Asia Minor and modern Turkey. Sayce recorded the story of his finds in the book *The Hittites, Story of a Forgotten Empire*. In 1906, Dr. Hugo Winckler, excavating at Boghos-Keui on the Halys River ninety miles east of Ankara, discovered the former capital and a treasure-trove of inscriptions on clay tablets in cuneiform script and written in the Babylonian and Hittite languages. It took some time to decipher the Hittite tongue, but it was accomplished. One very interesting find at Carchemish was a Hittite tablet on which the lines alternated, the first being written from left to right, the second from right to left, and so on.

In 1911, the archeologist Sir Leonard Woolley and T. E. Lawrence, later to become famous as Lawrence of Arabia, began excavations at Carchemish where they uncovered an immense quantity of material telling of a great empire which included all Asia west of the Euphrates River. There had been two great eras of expansion in the life of the Hittite Empire, one at the time of the first great Babylonian dynasty, around 1700 B.C., and the other from 1400–1200 B.C., when the Hittites are mentioned in the Tell el-Amarna letters. The earliest international treaty so far recovered is one signed between Ramses II of Egypt and Hattushilish II of the Hittite Empire—a treaty promising the maintenance of peace and harmony between them, a treaty cemented by the marriage of the daughter of Hattushilish to Pharoah Ramses II. In David's time we hear of a treaty between David and Toi, king of Hamath (II Samuel 8:9); in 717 B.C. the Hittite Empire was finally overthrown by the Assyrian conqueror Sargon II.

## PERIOD OF THE JUDGES

It is natural that a period when Israel was weak and divided should not yield a quantity of archeological remains, but such as there are only confirm the situation pictured in the Book of Judges. Everywhere the predominance of the Philistines and the weakness of the Israelites is evident. It is this age which marks the end of the Bronze Age and the beginning of the Iron Age. In Palestine, from about 4000 B.C. until around 1200 B.C., copper was the ordinary metal for tools and weapons. Tin was added toward the end of the era in making bronze. Before 1200 iron was a rare and precious metal, as valued as gold and silver. The earliest smiths were Hittites, who jealously guarded their secret smelting process; iron weapons gave the Hittites a distinct advantage over their enemies. Excavations show that for a long time the Philistines possessed iron weapons and chariots which they forbade to the Jews. In Joshua 17:16, the Israelites tell of their fear of the chariots of iron of their enemies; in Judges 4:3 is a reference to the nine hundred iron chariots of Sisera, who commanded the army of Jabin, king of Canaan. In contrast to Philistine homes with their superior art and their iron implements are the ruins of the Israelite homes devoid of all this. Their houses were crudely built and small. In I Samuel 13:19–22, we learn that there were no smiths among the Israelites, "lest the Hebrews make them swords and spears." In verse 22 only Saul and Jonathan had so much as a sword or a spear. Here again the Bible and the discoveries of archeology are fully in harmony.

It is worthy of note that the art of constructing waterproof cisterns spread rapidly among the Israelites, making possible settlements away from perennial streams or other sources of water, indeed possible wherever there was rain. The Israelites learned to coat the cisterns with lime plaster. It was during this period, about the beginning of the twelfth century, that the entire eastern shore of the Mediterranean was invaded by seafaring people, the Philistines, who captured the areas along the seashore and many cities farther inland. For centuries the Philistines were the main enemies of Israel, at one time capturing Shiloh and the ark of the Covenant. They brought with them a new and typical form of pottery similar to Cyprian ware and apparently originating in Greece. Jugs with a strainer spout have been found in large quantities, the spouts apparently being for the purpose of straining the husks out of beer. The great number of jugs found indicate a people who drank heavily. In the Book of Judges we read of drunken bouts in the story of Samson, who, it will be recalled, was a Nazarite from his youth and consecrated, and so prohibited from drinking wine, cutting his hair and touching a corpse. It was when the lords of the Philistines were holding a great feast in Gaza and "their hearts were merry" that they brought out Samson to make sport of him and he was given the opportunity to bring the temple crashing about their heads, so that "the dead which he slew at his death were more than they which he slew in his life" (Judges 16:30).

### THE POOL OF GIBEON

At the bottom of this 33-foot pit an American expedition discovered a well some 2,500 years old. It was reached by a spiral stairs of 79 steps. The pool is referred to in II Samuel as the scene of the battle between the rival houses of David and Saul.

# 8

# THE UNITED
# KINGDOM

AS RELATED IN THE BOOK OF I SAMUEL, THE FIRST KING OVER ISRAEL
was Saul and his first victory was gained at Michmash (I Samuel
14). By this victory he drove back the Philistines and won many
recruits to his cause of liberation. His headquarters were established at Gibeah, where excavations have brought to light a strong
fortress dating from Saul's period. Its exact size is not certain but
it was at least one hundred sixty-nine feet long and one hundred
fourteen feet wide. It is crude and simple in construction, but very
strong. Many bronze arrowheads and sling stones were found, evidence of the crudeness of that civilization. The end of Saul's reign
came at Mount Gilboa where, defeated by the Philistines, his sons
were killed and Saul himself fell upon his sword. Saul's head was
passed in triumph among the Philistines and sent to the temple
of Dagon in Bethshan. His armor was hung in the temple of Ashtaroth at Bethshan, and his body was nailed to its walls (I Chronicles 10:10). Excavations at Bethshan have uncovered one of the
most complete sites of ancient cities yet discovered. The pile of
ruins was seventy-nine feet high when excavations began, and no
less than eighteen different strata of buildings were uncovered,
running from 4000 B.C. down to the Middle Ages. In the city dating
from the time of David ruins of two temples were found, almost
certainly the temples of Dagon and Ashtaroth mentioned in the
Bible. The city had been burned at that time, probably by David in
revenge for the barbarities practiced on the body of King Saul.
Following the death of Saul and his sons, David ascended the
Israelite throne.

THE MIGHTY MOUND

Overlooking the Valley of the Jordan River, this mount once
Mt. Gilboa is believed to have taken place near here. It was in
Philistines. Later Bethshan was known as

OF BETHSHAN

supported the ancient city of Bethshan. The historic Battle of
this battle that King Saul and his three sons were killed by the
Scythopolis and today it is called Beisan.

Until the time of King David, Jerusalem was in the hands of the Jebusites. For centuries it had been an important city. The king Abdi-Hiba, who wrote some of the Tell el-Amarna letters, lived at Jerusalem, which was even then the capital and known as U-ru-salim. The name of the king, Abdi-Hiba, which means "slave of Hiba," shows that he was a Hittite, for Hiba was a Hittite goddess. It is a revelation of the cosmopolitan character of Palestine in the year 1400 to find that a Hittite king, living in Palestine, wrote letters in Babylonian cuneiform script and the Akkadian language to the king of Egypt! When David became king he was anxious to have his capital as near as possible to the northern tribes, who accepted his kingship reluctantly, so Jerusalem seemed a good choice to him, both for its northern location and its great natural system of defense. Indeed it was so strong that the Jebusites boasted it could be defended by the lame and the blind. Unfortunately the text of II Samuel 5:6–8 is on this point obscure so that the precise method by which the city was captured is uncertain. The King James version makes reference to a "gutter," the Revised Version to a "water shaft," by which David's forces were to enter the stronghold. If these are correct, doubtless the references are to an underground aqueduct which the earliest inhabitants of Jerusalem had carved under Mount Zion. This tunnel was discovered by Sir Charles Warren during one of the first archeological hunts in Jerusalem. It runs for some five hundred feet, from the spring now called the Fountain of the Virgin, located in the valley of Kidron, to an underground cave. From this cave a vertical shaft led to a platform at the top where women stood to draw water. From this platform a sloping passageway extended within the fortress walls. There was thus a secure source of water during times of siege. It may be that David's warriors followed this aqueduct from its source in the cave and climbed the shaft in order to enter the fortress. However, the Hebrew word has most recently been translated as "hook." Conceivably, the invaders may have scaled the fortress walls by means of hooks. Or the scaling hooks may have been used to ascend the inner shaft and take the fortress by surprise.

With Jerusalem as his fortress and capital, King David was able to enlarge his kingdom. But the remains of the fortresses which have been excavated at Tell Beit Mirsim, the ancient Debir, in southern Palestine and at Beth-shemesh, about fifteen miles west of Jerusalem, belong to the early days of David's reign. The glacis uncovered on the hill of Ophel, south of the temple of Jerusalem, is apparently Davidic as well. But David was more warrior than builder, so the remains of his times are few.

Archeological investigation also has helped to explain how it was possible for the little kingdom of Israel to expand so rapidly without opposition. Until the time of Ramses II, Egypt was the dominant power in Palestine and such a strong independent kingdom would not have been permitted to rise. But for many years none of the successors of Ramses II had amounted to much; they were pliant tools in the hands of the priests of Egypt. Domestic corruption increased and the empire became progressively weak. With the fall of the twentieth dynasty and the rise of the twenty-first, Egypt fell completely under priestly control and there were no attempts at foreign aggression. Hence Egypt was in no position to interfere with the plans and conquests of King David.

Similarly, the records of Babylon and Assyria reveal that for these empires it was a period of quiescence. King David had much local opposition and battles to fight, but he did not have to meet the might of Egypt, Babylonia or Assryia. The Hittites were undergoing a period of relative weakness, giving the Israelites a free hand as far as the banks of the Euphrates. King David conquered successively Edom, Ammon, Philistia and Amalek. His farthest conquest on the north was Zobah, which had been encroaching on the lands of Assyria and threatening that enfeebled kingdom. It may be owing to David that the Assyrian empire persisted, for he destroyed their most successful foe.

David was succeeded by his son Solomon, who was a great builder and left many relics of his reign. Remains of his buildings have been found in Megiddo, Gezer and Eglon (cf. I Kings 9:15–19). The excavations at Megiddo are particularly of note, the most extensive ever carried out in Palestine. Begun in 1925 under the auspices of the University of Chicago, excavating continued over a period of ten years. Four complete cities were explored and entirely removed, cities flourishing from the tenth to the fourth centuries B.C.

The ruined city on the top of the mound proved to be Babylonian and Persian, the one below it Assyrian, and the third and fourth, Israelite; the fourth represented the days of King Solomon. Here were extensive royal stables and the ruins of the palace built for the governor Baana, who was Solomon's appointee to rule the district. The stables were exceedingly well built and had room for about four

PHOTOGRAPH AND DRAWING OF IVORY PLAQUE SHOWING THE PRINCE OF
MEGIDDO RECEIVING PRISONERS AND TRIBUTE

hundred and fifty horses. The governor's residence was in a new
style, showing Phoenician influence, a style exactly duplicated in
ruins uncovered by R. S. Macalister, an English archeologist, at
Gezer, eighteen miles northwest of Jerusalem. Each of Solomon's
twelve governors was ordered to provide provisions for the king's
palace for one month of each year, and in consequence a large
amount of storage space was needed. Such was found to be the
case in Baana's palace which had very large store rooms. A later
exploration uncovered a subterranean treasury, dating from the
time of Ramses III, about 1200 B.C., and containing about two hundred carved and incised ivory pieces of rare beauty. Solomon's
interest in horses is mentioned in I Kings 10:26-29 and II Chronicles 1:14-17. The stables found in Megiddo were composed of
units built on a standard plan. Stone pillars separated the horses

and served as hitching posts. Stone mangers for their food were provided and the ground paved with rough stone to prevent slipping. Similar stables from the same age have been found at Bethshan, Hazor and Ta'annak.

Gezer also is the site of the only Hebrew inscription of that day so far uncovered. It apparently dates from the reign of Solomon or slightly after, around 925 B.C., and is known as the Gezer calendar. On the limestone tablet was inscribed the periods of the agricultural year in the form of a simple and easily remembered rhyme which bears some resemblance to our "Thirty days hath September." The rhyme has been of some aid in dating the Twenty-eighth Psalm and a number of the oracles of Baalam.

King Solomon's temple was completely destroyed and no traces of it have been found. Probably it was not very large, no more than a hundred feet long and thirty feet wide, and made of stone covered with cedar inlaid with gold. Within was the holy of holies, one of two rooms, in which cherubim stood guard over the ark of the Covenant. Outside the temple was a huge brass sea, a bowl about fifteen feet in diameter and seven and a half feet high, cast in the Jordan Valley by workmen sent by King Hiram of Tyre. Computation has shown that such a bronze bowl must have weighed between twenty-five and thirty tons. The sea and two mammoth brass pillars stood in front of the temple (I Kings 7).

There has been much discussion of the exact form of the temple; the description in the Bible is detailed but by no means clear. It would be a great help if some contemporary temple were unearthed in Palestine, but so far this has not occurred, although some small shrines have been reconstructed. Recent excavations adjoining a royal palace at Tell Tainat in Syria have uncovered the remains of an eighth-century B.C. temple strikingly similar to Biblical descriptions of Solomon's temple. The bases of two large pillars stand at the entryway, and there is a larger outer room and a smaller room as a shrine. From this it is possible to picture Solomon's temple.

King Solomon, with the aid of King Hiram of Tyre, built a fleet at Ezion-geber on the Red Sea. Excavations at Ezion-geber have brought to light a hitherto unknown phase of Solomon's activities. A huge smelter, in which both copper and iron were refined, the largest ever found in the Near East, has been uncovered. Nearby were great walled camps for the slave workers. The smelter was so built as to take the maximum advantage of the winds that blow down the valley of the Arabah River, and employed some of the principles of a modern smelter. In Deuteronomy 8:9 the Israelites are told they will have a land in whose hills are metals. There are indeed large quantities of minerals in the hills of Edom and the Arabah, where the ruins of many mines have been uncovered. These ruins show that the region, today entirely a desert, in Solomon's time had hundreds of towns and villages and was thickly populated. The minerals were partially refined at the mine heads and then sent to Ezion-geber for the final stages of production.

King Solomon was impoverished by his mighty cities, fleets and mines and was forced to turn over to King Hiram twenty Galilean cities, as told in I Kings 9:10, in payment for his aid. Solomon's expansive program necessitated harsh measures and heavy taxation; immediately upon his death the people demanded of Rehoboam, his son, an easing of the tax burden. Rehoboam consulted first with his father's old advisors and then with his young friends, and took the advice of the latter, refusing to cut the taxes (I Kings 12:1–20). As a result of his folly, ten of the twelve tribes of Solomon refused to accept Rehoboam's rule and set up their own kingdom under their own king. They never again were united with the two tribes of Judah and Benjamin that remained loyal to Rehoboam. The long period of freedom from foreign interference came to an end as a new aggressive dynasty rose in Egypt under King Shishak (or Sheshonk), the founder of the twenty-second Egyptian dynasty. In I Kings 14:25–26, King Shishak is described as coming to Jerusalem and carrying off all of the vast treasure that had been accumulated by King Solomon. King Shishak has left on record at Karnak his own account of his victories over the Israelites (about 920 B.C.). The god Amun is shown in relief, drawing by a cord rows of Semitic captives, doubtless Hebrews. On the entire relief no less than one hundred fifty-six captives are represented, each one of whom symbolizes a different Hebrew town or city that Shishak claimed to have captured. A dozen of the legible names are names of cities mentioned in the Old Testament. One of the places captured is identified as the "Field of Abram." Thus Shishak's presence and victories in Palestine in the time of Rehoboam are fully confirmed. The Karnak record shows that northern Israel was also invaded, a fact not mentioned in the Bible.

# 9

# THE NORTHERN KINGDOM

IN THE NORTHERN KINGDOM THE RULER WHO LEFT THE MOST LASTING imprint on history and archeology was Omri, an army officer who seized the throne (I Kings 16:15–24). Though he ruled for but twelve years, a century later the Assyrians spoke of the Kings of Israel as the House of Omri. The capital of Omri's kingdom was Samaria, which has yielded a quantity of valuable archeological remains. Jeroboam, the founder of the northern kingdom, had made his capital first at Shechem and later at Tirzah. But Omri selected a new and more formidable location because of its centrality and its defensibility. Samaria is not an old site. Located on the top of a mountain, it was originally considered an impractical place to build a large city—before the people learned to construct waterproof cisterns for the storage of rain water. Archeology has confirmed what the Bible records, that Omri was the first to erect a city on the mountain of Samaria.

The name Samaria means *watch mountain*. Ideally located, in the center of the kingdom of Israel, it made a splendid new capital which in time was so strongly fortified as to be practically impregnable. Excavations on the site of the old city were first undertaken by George A. Reisner and others sent out by Harvard University in 1908–1910. Later in 1931–1933, and again in 1935, the excavations were enlarged. Six different layers were uncovered, dating from Omri's time into the eighth century. Omri, and later his son Ahab, leveled the top of the mountain, three hundred and thirty feet above the plain, and with geometrical precision built strong outer and inner walls. Later kings built walls on the middle terrace and on the lower slopes. In II Kings 6:24–31 we read of famine in Samaria, caused by a siege so severe that cannibalism was resorted to, yet the city was not taken; and in II Kings 17:5–6 the city of Samaria was besieged for three years by the Assyrians before it surrendered. Excavations have revealed a number of large rock-cut cisterns. The oldest Hebrew palace was on the western brow of the hill overlooking the Mediterranean, a relatively simple building. The ruins of much more elaborate palaces have been discovered. A strong rectangular tower stood at the end of the outer court and a cemented pool, thirty-three feet long and nearly seventeen feet wide, that may well be the pool where Ahab's blood-stained chariot was washed, as told in I Kings 22:38. The next verse describes Ahab's ivory palace. Archeologists did find that a second palace was decorated with numerous ivory plaques and panels. In the palace an alabaster vase was found inscribed with the name of Osorkon II, a contemporary of King Ahab, which further identifies the palace as that of King Ahab. Apparently the ivory panels were fastened to the furniture or hung on the walls. Many subjects are pictured on the ivory panels, lotus, lilies, papyrus, palmettes, lions, bulls, deer, winged figures, sphynxes, gods of Egypt and the like, confirming the strong Egyptian influence of the time. One beautiful example of these ivories is a representation of the infant god Horus sitting on a lotus blossom and holding a flail. The lavish decoration provides striking illustration of the luxury denounced by the eighth-century prophet Amos, who described the inhabitants of Samaria as people who "lie upon beds of ivory" (Amos 6:4) and predicted that "the houses of ivory shall perish" (Amos 3:15). The remains of an ivory bed were found in northern Syria at Arslan Tash. One of the pieces bore the name of Hazael, king of Damascus, to whom there are many references in the books of Kings and Chronicles. In Samaria, ostraca or written potsherds were uncovered, probably from the reign of Jeroboam II, who ruled early in the eighth century. They contain accounts of receipts of revenue by the king. "In the tenth year from Azza to Goddiyo, a jar of fine oil." Compare again Amos' denunciation in Chapter 6:6. He says that the rulers of Samaria "drink wine from bowls and anoint themselves with the chief ointments; but they are not grieved for the affliction of Joseph." The names on the ostraca are significant. Some contain the name of Baal in combination as Mari-

baal. Others contain the name Yahu, reflecting the conflict between the two religions which the prophet Amos deplored and denounced.

One of the most striking finds bearing on the history of this
period is the so-called Moabite stone. It was discovered by a German missionary, F. A. Klein, at a place called Dibon, north of the
river Arnon and east of the Dead Sea. It was partially buried in the
earth, but Klein was able to copy some words from it and bring it
to the attention of scholars. The stone was of a bluish-black basalt,
two feet wide, nearly four feet high and fourteen and one half
inches thick, and rounded at the top and bottom. An inscription in
Phoenician letters, some thirty-four lines, had been carved on the
stone. Klein was authorized to negotiate the purchase of the stone
for the Prussian government and reached an agreement with the
Arabs to pay approximately forty dollars for it. The French government had heard of the stone and sent an agent to make a
"squeeze" (facsimile impression) of the carvings and to negotiate
for its purchase. They offered the equivalent of fifteen hundred
dollars for the stone. These competing offers stirred the cupidity of
the Arabs, who decided the stone must have some magical proper-
ties. They built a fire to heat the stone, poured cold water on it,
shattered the great stone and distributed the fragments as talismans. It was only with great difficulty and at great expense that
most of the fragments were recovered. They were pieced together
and the stone is now to be seen in the Louvre.

The inscription on the Moabite stone remarkably supplements
the story told in the third chapter of II Kings, although the story
of the revolt is not mentioned in the Bible. The inscription makes
no reference to the victory of Ahab which the Bible records, but
names, cities mentioned and the general situation is the same. The
language in which it is written is a valuable link in our understanding of development of the Semitic languages. The Moabite stone
records that after Omri had overrun Moab, Ahab, his son, was wont
to collect an annual tribute of 100,000 rams. After Ahab's death,
Mesha refused to continue paying this tribute. He was driven by
King Jehoram into his fortress of Kir-hareseth, where he sacrificed
his own son on the top of the city wall as an offering to Chemosh
his god. Thereafter, he reports, he was able to defeat Jehoram in
a series of battles and to expel Israel from Moab. "Now the men
of Gad had always dwelt in the land of Ataroth, and the king of

THE MOABITE STONE

The inscription—in a language akin to Hebrew—remarkably supplements
the third chapter of II Kings.

Israel had built Ataroth for them; but I fought against the town and took it and slew all the people of the town as satiation [intoxication] for Chemosh and Moab."* Cities and fortresses of Moab were restored and strengthened. Previous defeats were attributed to the anger of their gods and these victories attributed to their assistance. The inscription mentions the name of Yahweh, to whom Israel is said to have erected a shrine in Nebo, and many of the towns and cities of the Old Testament. Altogether this is the finest inscription in a language akin to Hebrew yet found. Actually the language and idiom are nearly the same as that of the Old Testament. It reveals how advanced was the civilization of Moab in the ninth century B.C. Ironically, its only error is the boast that as a result of the Moab victories "Israel perished forever."

It was during the reign of Ahab, son of Omri, that Israel first came into contact with the threat from the east of the new and growing Assyrian power. It is probably the appearance of this threat which explains Ahab's surprising gentleness toward Syria (1 Kings Chapter 20). Ahab defeated King Benhadad of Damascus, but did not kill him or destroy the capital city of Damascus, as was the practice in those days. Instead, Ahab formed an alliance, taking back some of the cities which had formerly belonged to Israel in the days of Omri and certain streets in Damascus. Why should he have done this? Probably he was statesman enough to realize that Syria was the last bulwark between Israel and Assyria; that if Syria passed away his kingdom would be open at once to the Assyrian invasion. The destruction of Damascus would be suicide. Instead, as Assyrian inscriptions inform us, Ahab allied his forces with his recent Syrian foes to ward off the threat of invasion.

Shalmaneser III, who reigned 859–825, left a record of the Syrian-Israeli coalition. In his account of the first of his twenty-one campaigns of conquest, he describes the crossing of the Euphrates River and the conquest of Aleppo. He relates how a coalition of twelve kings was formed to fight against him and gives the forces which each of these brought to the battle. It appears that the two strongest kings were Benhadad of Damascus and Ahab of Israel. Shalmaneser gives Benhadad's forces as being composed of 1,200 chariots, 1,200 cavalry and 20,000 soldiers; and Ahab's as being 2,000 chariots and 10,000 soldiers. Shalmaneser reports: "I fought

* Pritchard, *op. cit.,* p. 320.

with them with [the support of] the mighty forces of Ashur, which Ashur, my lord, has given to me, and the strong weapons which Nergal, my leader, has presented to me, [and] I did inflict a defeat upon them between the towns Karkara and Gilzau. I slew 14,000 of their soldiers with the sword, descending upon them like Adad when he makes a rainstorm pour down. I spread their corpses [everywhere], filling the entire plain with their widely scattered [fleeing] soldiers. During the battle I made their blood flow down the *hur-pa-lu* of the district."* In another inscription Shalmaneser claims that in this battle he killed 20,500; in yet another inscription he puts the figure at 25,000. Actually the battle seems to have been little more than a draw. Shalmaneser returned at once to Nineveh and did not return to this area for five years.

A later inscription, detailing the account of Shalmaneser's sixteenth campaign, is of special interest.

In the eighteenth year of my rule, I crossed the Euphrates for the sixteenth time. Hazael of Damascus [mentioned in I Kings 19: 15, 17 and in II Kings 8] put his trust in his numerous army and called up his troops in great number. He made Senir, a mountain facing Lebanon, his fortress. I fought with him and defeated him. Sixteen thousand of his soldiers I cut down with arms, 1,121 of his chariots, 470 of his cavalry with his camp I took from him. To save his life he fled. I pursued him. In Damascus, his royal city, I shut him up. His parks I cut down. As far as the mountains of Hauren I marched. Towns without number I laid waste; I devastated, burned with fire. Their innumerable spoil I carried away. At that time I received the tribute of the Tyrians, the Sidonians, of Jehu, son of Omri.

Not only has Shalmaneser III left us a record of his campaign, but on the famous Black Obelisk, which Sir Austen Layard found at Calah, he has left us pictures of various defeated powers bringing tribute, among whom he includes Jehu, son of Omri. Shalmaneser, attended by his aides, receives obeisance. Directly in front of him is Jehu, or his representative, bowing low to the earth. Four Hebrew officials follow and thirteen Hebrew porters bearing gifts. These are described on the obelisk as follows: "Tribute of Jehu, son of Omri; silver, gold, a bowl of gold, chalices of gold, cups of gold, bars of lead, scepters for the hand of the king and balsam wood, I

* *Ibid.*, p. 279.

THE BLACK OBELISK OF SHALMANESER III

The obelisk—now in the British Museum—is inscribed with the
expeditions undertaken during the thirty-one years of his reign.

received from him." This is the earliest picture of the Hebrews yet found in Assyria.

Nevertheless, shortly afterward Assyria performed a great service to Israel by destroying its dangerous enemy, Syria. In II Kings 10:32–33 and II Kings 13:3–7 the kings Hazael and Benhadad win a series of victories over Israel, capturing many cities and towns. Then came the Assyrian king Adad-nirari III, who ruled 812–782, and conquered the area and despoiled Damascus. This is his record of conquest:

I marched against the country *Sa-imerisus:* I shut up Mari', king of Damascus (*Imerisu*) in Damascus (*Di-ma-as-qi*), his royal residence. The terror-inspiring glamor of Ashur, my [text: his] lord, overwhelmed him and he seized my feet assuming the position of a slave [of mine.] [Then] I received in his [own] Palace in Damascus, his royal residence, 2,300 talents of silver [corresponding to] 20 talents of gold, 5,000 talents of iron, garments of linen with multi-colored trimmings, a bed [inlaid] with ivory, a *nimattu*-couch mounted and inlaid with ivory, [and] countless [other objects being] his possesions.*

Following Adad-nirari's reign came three weak Assyrian kings, which relieved the pressure on Israel and allowed time for recovery.

Both Israel and Judah prospered and expanded their territories. Jeroboam II of Israel, the fourth king of the Jehu dynasty, expanded the borders of his kingdom from Hamath to the Euphrates and east of the Dead Sea. At the same time, Judah, under the rule of the able King Uzziah, or Azariah, conquered Philistia and enjoyed a period of great activity in building and agriculture. An interesting relic of Uzziah's reign has been found on the site of Elath, which, as we learn in II Chronicles, was reconquered by his army. The relic is a beautifully carved seal bearing the inscription "belonging to Jotham," who may well have been Uzziah's son of that name who became regent after his father contracted leprosy.

Following these weaker kings, Pul of Assyria, calling himself Tiglathpileser, seized the Assyrian throne and resumed wars of aggression. In II Kings 15:19–20, Menahem gives to Pul a thousand talents of silver in return for his support of his kingship. Pul himself reports that he received tribute from Rezoin of Damascus, Menahem of Samaria, Hiram of Tyre and others, "gold, silver, tin, iron,

* *Ibid.*, pp. 281-282.

elephant-hides, ivory, linen garments with multicolored trimmings, blue-dyed wool, purple-dyed wool, ebony-wood, boxwood-wood, whatever was precious [enough for a] royal treasure; also lambs whose stretched hides were dyed purple, [and] wild birds whose spread-out wings were dyed blue, [furthermore] horses, mules, large and small cattle, [male] camels, female camels with their foals."* Whatever additional gifts Menahem may have made, the silver alone (at today's valuation) would be worth a million and a half dollars. II Kings 15:30 tells how Hoshea conspired against the Israelite king Pekeh, and slew him. Pul records: "They overthrew their king Pekah (*Pa-qu-ha*) and I placed Hosea (*A-u-si-'*) as king over them." It was King Pul who commenced the policy of deportations which later kings pursued. In II Kings 15:29, Pul carries off captives from many of the cities of Galilee and Naphtali to his own city in Assyria.

In II Kings 16:7–10, Ahaz, king of Judah, sends a gift to Tiglath-pileser, beseeching him to come to his aid by fighting against Syria. Pul captured the city of Damascus, killed its king Rezoin and carried its people into captivity. Thus he conquered a people that his predecessors had striven to take for a hundred years, fulfilling the prophecy of Isaiah 7:16 that Damascus should speedily be without her kings. In the inscriptions of Tiglathpileser we find the name of Ahaz listed among those who were subject to his rule. The only other contemporary reference to Ahaz is found on a seal which is inscribed "to Ushna, servant of Ahaz." It is a beautifully wrought carnelian seal in the shape of a scarab.

According to II Kings 17:3–6, Tiglathpileser was succeeded by Shalmaneser V, who besieged Samaria. Apparently he died shortly thereafter. Before the capture of Samaria, Sargon II had ascended the throne, for in the inscriptions we find him claiming credit for the conquest of Samaria:

At the begi(nning of my royal rule, I . . . the town of the Sama) rians [I besieged, conquered] (two lines destroyed) [for the god . . . who le]t me achieve [this] my triumph. . . . I led away as prisoners [27,290 inhabitants of it [and] [equipped] from among [them (soldiers to man)] fifty chariots for my royal corps . . . (the town I) re[built] better than [it was] before and [settled] therein people from countries which [I] myself [had con]quered. I placed an officer

* *Ibid.*, p. 283.

of mine as governor over them and imposed upon them tribute as (is customary) for Assyrian citizens.

I besieged and conquered Samaria (*Sa-me-ri-na*), led away as booty 27,290 inhabitants of it. I formed from among them a contingent of fifty chariots and made remaining [inhabitants] assume their [social] positions. I installed over them an officer of mine and imposed upon them the tribute of the former king.*

In II Kings 17:24–41, we find full confirmation of Sargon's account and the story of how he brought people from his own kingdom to settle in Samaria and mingle with the people who remained. Most of the ten tribes of Israel did not leave their homeland. It is a mistake to inquire what became of the "lost ten tribes." They were not lost; but in the course of time they were absorbed into the surrounding populations by intermarriage. Sargon's victory marks an end to the history of Israel. It never again existed as an independent kingdom. The Samaritans were a separate and hated race in the time of Jesus, and today no more than a few hundred remain of this once proud people.

* *Ibid.*, pp. 284-285.

# 10

# THE LAST DAYS OF THE KINGDOM OF JUDAH

## The Glory of Old Babylon

SARGON II WAS SUCCEEDED BY THE MIGHTY KING SENNACHERIB. HE has left on record the story of his campaign against Judah, which is described from the Jewish side in II Kings 18:13, 19:36. His account is as follows:

I assaulted Ekron and killed the officials and patricians who had committed the crime and hung their bodies on poles surrounding the city. The (common) citizens who were guilty of minor crimes, I considered prisoners of war. The rest of them, those who were not accused of crimes and misbehavior, I released. . . .

As to Hezekiah, the Jew, he did not submit to my yoke, I laid siege to 46 of his strong cities, walled forts, and to the countless small villages in their vicinity, and conquered [them] by means of well-stamped [earth-] ramps, and battering-rams brought [thus] near [to the walls] [combined with] the attack by foot soldiers, [using] mines, breaches, as well as sapper work. I drove out [of them] 200,150 people, young and old, male and female, horses, mules, donkeys, camels, big and small cattle beyond counting, and considered [them] booty. Himself I made a prisoner in Jerusalem, his royal residence, like a bird in a cage. I surrounded him with earthwork in order to molest those who were leaving his city's gate. His towns which I had plundered, I took away from his country and gave them [over] to Mitinti, king of Ashdod, Padi, king of Ekron, and Sillibel, king of Gaza. Thus I reduced his country but I still increased the tribute and the *katrû*-presents [due] to me [as his] overlord which I imposed [later] upon him beyond the former tribute, to be delivered annually. Hezekiah himself, whom the terror-inspiring splendor of my lordship had overwhelmed and whose irregular and elite troops which he had brought into Jerusalem, his royal residence, in order to strengthen [it], had deserted him, did send me, later, to Nineveh, my lordly city, together with 30 talents of gold, 800 talents of silver, precious stones, antimony, large cuts of red stone, couches (inlaid) with ivory, nîmedu-chairs (inlaid) with ivory, elephant-hides, ebony-wood, boxwood [and] all kinds of valuable treasures, his [own] daughters, concubines, male and female musicians. In order to deliver the tribute and to do obeisance as a slave he sent his [personal] messenger.*

In II Kings 18:13-16 we read of how Hezekiah gave tribute to Sennacherib, the amount there being given as thirty talents of gold and three hundred talents of silver. In II Kings 19:35 is the story of how the angel of the Lord passed through the Assyrian camp at night and slew 185,000 of his men, so that the king rose up and fled to his own country. Nothing of this is mentioned in the Assyrian account. It is not surprising: ancient monarchs, like modern ones, tended to record not their failures but their successes. It would be highly unlikely that Sennacherib would leave a record of such a disaster and of so hasty a flight. It is to be noted, however, that in his own account Sennacherib does not claim to have taken Jerusalem; he has simply shut up Hezekiah "like a bird in a cage." Although Sennacherib reigned on for twenty years, he never again launched a campaign against Judah. It is as though some dread memory of disaster stayed his hand. Herodotus in his history tells of a vast Assyrian army moving against the Egyptians who came out to repel him in great force. Herodotus says that the Assyrians were overrun by field mice who so ate up their bowstrings and gnawed apart their leather trappings that they were left helpless and weaponless and so fled back to their own land. Probably this tradition had some basis in fact and echoes a disaster that occurred to the Assyrian army.

The mention of mice has led some to think that the direct cause of the disaster to the Assyrian hosts was the bubonic plague, as that is known to be transmitted by the fleas on rats. In any event Herodotus confirms the Biblical account of an overwhelming defeat. It is this event that inspired Lord Byron's "The Destruction of Sennacherib."

* Ibid., p. 288.

The Assyrian came down like the wolf on the fold,
And his cohorts were gleaming in purple and gold;
And the sheen of their spears was like stars on the sea,
When the blue waves roll nightly on deep Galilee.

Like the leaves of the forest when Summer is green,
That host with their banners at sunset were seen:
Like the leaves of the forest when Autumn hath blown,
That host on the morrow lay wither'd and strown.

For the Angel of Death spread his wings on the blast,
And breathed in the face of the foe as he pass'd;
And the eyes of the sleepers wax'd deadly and chill,
And their hearts but once heaved, and for ever grew still!

The siege of Lachish occurred just before this event and is of unusual interest because of the fine series of carved stone pictures of
that event which Sir Austen Layard uncovered at Nineveh in 1850.
A series of pictures carved on thirteen stone slabs illustrates the
siege and capture of this old fortress. Over them are written the
words: "Sennacherib, king of the world, king of Assyria, sat upon
a *nîmedu*-throne and passed in review the booty [taken] from
Lachish (*La-ki-su*)."* The walls of the city of Lachish are pictured
on the summit of a steep mound. There are towers and projections
with small barred windows; wooden railings and what look like
round shields project from the parapet of the towers. There are
fortified outworks in the neighborhood of the entrance and a sally
port or water tower about halfway down the mound. The surrounding country is represented as hilly and wooded. The walls and
towers are alive with defenders shooting stones and arrows at the
attackers. One can count no less than ten siege mounds which the
attackers have raised against the steep glacis protecting the walls.
These are built of bricks, stone, soil, and the trunks of trees. There
are seven battering rams rolled up to the walls on these runways.
Each of the siege engines is mounted on four wheels and is leather-
covered with a hood in front. Each shelters three men—one to work
the battering ram or to use a crowbar with a point to pick stones out
of the walls; another to shoot arrows from under cover of the hood;
and a third to pour water from a long-handled ladle on the fire-

* *Ibid.*

brands which the defenders rain down on the primitive tank. Upon this bas-relief everything is happening at once; the investment, the siege, the assault and the surrender. Archers are kneeling in the front ranks, in the next they are bending forward, and in the third they are standing upright, all portrayed as discharging arrows at the city's defenders. Shield-bearers with wicker shields covered with hide are there to protect the archers, who also take shelter behind the tanks. There are slingers and spearmen. Ladders set up for escalading are tumbling from the walls; in a desperate effort to check the advance, the besieged are casting their chariots down on the heads of the attackers. That the city was captured is attested to by both the Biblical account and that of Sennacherib.

In excavating the city of Lachish, archeologists have uncovered what is a most impressive engineering feat of primitive craftsmen— a huge pit cut from solid limestone, eighty-four by seventy-four feet in area and eighty-five feet deep. It is amazing how over 500,000 cubic feet of rock could thus have been cut in a day when there was no modern machinery or explosives and when tools were made of flint, copper and soft iron. Seemingly this pit was for water storage, but there is still some uncertainty on this score.

Another striking engineering feat of that day is Hezekiah's tunnel from the Gihon spring. The tunnel is mentioned briefly in II Kings 20:20. It was cleaned out by the Parker expedition, together with other ancient waterways, in the years 1909–1911. It averages about six feet in height and is over eighteen hundred feet long. A native boy, wading in the tunnel, noticed some scratches on the side of the wall which were reported to those outside. Archeologists have translated the writing and find it reads as follows:

[. . . when] (the tunnel) was driven through. And this was the way in which it was cut through: While [. . . ] (were) still [. . .] axe (s), each man toward his fellow, and while they were still three cubits to be cut through, [there was heard] the voice of a man calling to his fellow, for there was *an overlap* in the rock on the right [and on the left]. And when the tunnel was driven through the quarry men hewed [the rock[, each man toward his fellow, axe against axe; and the water flowed from the spring toward the reservoir for 1,200 cubits, and the height of the rock above the head(s) of the quarry-men was 100 cubits. °

° *Ibid.*, p. 321.

This inscription was cut out by an unauthorized person and is now preserved in a museum at Constantinople. At the time of its construction, the spring was outside the city walls. It was concealed by rocks piled over it, and the water was brought by this tunnel to a point within the city walls.

Following the assassination of Sennacherib, related both in II Kings 19:37 and in the inscriptions, Esar-haddon his son reigned in his stead. He became the greatest conqueror of them all and succeeded in subjugating faraway Egypt. In his records he tells of demanding from western kings, including Manasseh, king of Judah, timber and stones for building his palace at Nineveh.

His successor Ashurbanipal tells of putting down a rebellion in the west, and also names Manasseh as a vassal king. In II Chronicles 33:10-13, Manasseh is taken as a prisoner to Babylon and later is restored to his throne. This captivity may be what is reflected in an inscription left by Esar-haddon which reads as follows:

I called up the kings of the country Hatti and (of the region) on the other side of the river [Euphrates] (to wit): Ba'lu, king of Tyre, Manasseh (*Me-na-si-i*), king of Judah (Ia-u-di), . . . 12 kings from the seacoast; . . . ten kings from Cyprus (*Iadnana*) amidst the sea, together 22 kings of Hatti, the seashore and the islands; all these I sent out and made them transport under terrible difficulties, to Nineveh, the town (where I exercise) my rulership, as building material for my palace: big logs, long beams (and) thin boards from cedar and pine trees, products of the Sirara and Lebanon (*Lab-na-na*) mountains, which had grown for a long time into tall and strong timber, (also) from their quarries [lit: place of creation] in the mountains, statues of protective deities (etc.). . . . *

Manasseh's restoration is not mentioned in the inscriptions, but a parallel incident is recorded: Pharaoh Necho was taken a prisoner to Babylon and later restored to his former seat of power. Ashurbanipal devoted his later years to collecting books and created a great library which was found by Rassam in 1852.

Following the reign of Ashurbanipal Assyria's strength rapidly declined. In 612 B.C. a coalition of the Babylonians and Medes captured the Assyrian capital of Nineveh, and shortly after at the battle of Carchemish finally defeated the combined armies of the Egyptians and Assyrians. The destruction of the city of Nineveh is

* *Ibid.*, p. 291.

vividly portrayed in the prophecies of Nahum, chapters 2, 3—
prophecies that were literally fulfilled.

## The Glory of Old Babylon

The excavation of the ruins of old Babylon began comparatively
recently. It was in 1898 that the German archeologist, Robert
Koldewey, commenced operations on that site. In contrast to Sir
Austen Layard and Paul Botta, who had no idea of what they might
find, Koldewey knew a great deal of the history and buildings of old
Babylon and was confident that he would be able to uncover relics
of the time of Nebuchadnezzar, whose achievements had come to
light on the Assyrian tablets.

It was not long before Koldewey had uncovered the truly tre-
mendous walls of the ancient city. For over fifteen years he worked
steadily with a force of three hundred diggers to reveal the ruins.
Thousands of tons of rubble had to be removed, in some instances
as much as seventy-seven feet in depth. Koldewey discovered that
an area of twelve square miles had been enclosed by double walls,
the outer more than twenty-two feet thick and the inner twenty-
five feet, built over thirty-eight feet apart. The space between the
walls was filled in so that on top of the walls there was a broad
highway sufficient for four pairs of horses to drive abreast. Regularly spaced watch towers gave the guards a still higher vantage
point from which to view the countryside. The watch towers were
about one hundred and sixty feet apart, there being three hundred
and sixty of them on the inner walls and two hundred and fifty on
the outer walls. Nebuchadnezzar's own description of this mighty
work was found to be as follows:

I caused a mighty wall to circumscribe Babylon in the east. I dug
its moats; and its escarpments I built out of bitumen and kiln brick.
At the edge of the moat I built a powerful wall as high as a hill. I
gave it wide gates and set in doors of cedarwood sheathed with copper. So that the enemy, who would evil, would not threaten the
sides of Babylon. I surrounded them with mighty floods as the bil-
lows of the sea flood the land. . . . This bastion I strengthened cun-
ningly, and of the city of Babylon made a fortress.°

° Quoted in C. W. Ceram, *Gods, Graves and Scholars* (New York: Knopf, 1951),
p. 284.

BABYLON, A PAINTING BY MAURICE BARDIN, SHOWING THE
RECONSTRUCTION OF THE CITY WITH THE ISHTAR GATE IN THE FOREGROUND

The excavations revealed that where his predecessors had used adobe Nebuchadnezzar introduced burnt bricks in his many buildings. He repaired more than twenty temples, and so huge is the quantity of bricks which bear his seal that most of the city of Hilleh has been built of them and a modern dam diverting the Euphrates River is largely constructed of Nebuchadnezzar's bricks. Among interesting objects from that age which Koldewey discovered were the vaulted arches and stone construction which apparently are the foundations of the famous hanging gardens of Babylon, one of the wonders of the ancient world. A triple shaft, evidently for raising water to the gardens, was found. The great artificial garden was planted on a tall brick platform in the very center of the city.

In Genesis II: 3–4 we read of the great tower of Babylon. From the ruins uncovered it appears that the original tower had been destroyed as early as the time of Hammurabi and another tower erected on its site. King Nabopolassar of Babylon has left a record of his work of rebuilding the tower: "At that time Marduk [his god] commanded me to build the Tower of Babel, which had become weakened by time and had fallen into disrepair; he commanded me to ground its base securely on the breast of the underworld, whereas its pinnacles should strain upwards to the skies."* Then his son, Nebuchadnezzar, supplemented his work, leaving a record which reads: "To raise up the top of E-temen-an-ki that it might rival heaven, I laid to my hand."† When completed the tower was formed of seven superimposed terraces reaching to a height of two hundred and eighty-eight feet and was two hundred and eighty-eight feet square at the base. No less than fifty-eight million bricks went into it, the vast work being completed by slaves. On the top there was a blue-tiled temple to Marduk which was empty but for a couch. Herodotus tells us that the Babylonians believed that Marduk would sometimes come there at night to rest. A marvelous view of the plain for many miles around was to be seen from the temple. In a large room at the bottom of the tower was a gigantic golden statue of Marduk. It was eighteen feet high and was made of eight hundred talents of gold (about eighteen tons, worth, at today's prices, about twenty-four million dollars).

Another striking feature of old Babylon was the Ishtar gate leading to the avenue where processions were held. This magnificent

* *Ibid.*, p. 288.
† *Ibid.*, p. 289.

avenue, seventy-three feet in width, was perfectly straight and flanked on both sides by a twenty-two-foot wall on which there was a striking frieze of one hundred and twenty lions, all in color. It must have afforded a magnificent sight when stately processions moved through the gateway. In the book of Daniel is Nebuchadnezzar's proud boast: "Is not this great Babylon, that I have built for the house of the kingdom by the might of my power, and for the honour of my majesty?" (Daniel 4:30) At the same time he professed devotion to the gods he worshiped: "When Marduk, the mighty Lord, promoted me to the lordship of the land and called me an exalted name that I might maintain the cities and renew the temples, I, prayerful, wise, suppliant worshiper of his godhead, bethought myself of the building up of that house." And again: "Oh Marduk, lord of the gods, my divine creator, before thee may my deeds be righteous, may they endure forever. Life for many generations, abundant prosperity, a secure throne, a long reign, grant as thy gift."

From the record in II Kings, we learn that Jerusalem underwent two sieges by Nebuchadnezzar and his armies. The first, when Jehoiachin was king, is related in Chapter 24:12-16. Apparently Jehoiachin had revolted against Nebuchadnezzar; in the eighth year of the Hebrew king's reign, the city was besieged, Jehoiachin taken captive and a vast quantity of loot carried away to Babylon— "all the treasures of the house of the Lord, and the treasures of the king's house, and cut in pieces all the vessels of gold which Solomon king of Israel had made in the temple of the Lord, as the Lord had said." In addition he carried off to enrich his capital city skilled artisans, "ten thousand captives, and all the craftsmen and smiths: none remained, save the poorest sort of the people in the land." With the publication in 1956 of four newly discovered tablets of the Babylonian Chronicle we have, for the first time, an extra-Biblical account of that crushing disaster.

Nebuchadnezzar appointed to reign in his stead Zedekiah, whom he evidently expected to be an obedient vassal. But Zedekiah was perplexed by a most dramatic and disturbing difference of opinion on the part of his prophets. The extraordinary tale is related in the Book of Jeremiah, chapters 27-28. On the one side stood Jeremiah himself, who, at the Lord's command, made for himself a heavy yoke and wore it in the streets, proclaiming that his nation and the surrounding nations must submit to the yoke of King Nebuchad-

These ruins are all that remain of the once magnificent city where
interpreted

BABYLON

King Belshazzar saw the "handwriting on the wall" in the dream by Daniel.

nezzar or perish. On the other hand was Hananiah the prophet, who "took the yoke from off the neck of Jeremiah and brake it" and predicted that even so would Yahweh break the yoke of Nebuchadnezzar within two years. Jeremiah in his turn made an unbreakable yoke of iron, warned that the nations had been given over to Nebuchadnezzar and predicted that Hananiah would die because of his lying prophecies. Torn between these contradictory predictions, it is not surprising that Zedekiah believed the more pleasing prophecy of deliverance and proceeded to ally himself with the king of Egypt and rebel against Nebuchadnezzar. Once again in 587 B.C. Jerusalem was besieged. After the long siege, and driven to desperation by hunger, Zedekiah and his warriors fled by night and made for the plains of the Jordan. There they were overtaken. Zedekiah's sons were slain before his eyes, he was blinded and carried in fetters to Babylon and the temple and fine buildings of Jerusalem were burned. The city walls were torn down and the remnant of the people of Jerusalem were carried away into captivity.

One of the most striking confirmations of the details of this story has to do with Jehoiachin, the prisoner king of Babylon. "Evil Merodach king of Babylon in the year that he began to reign did lift up the head of Jehoiachin king of Judah out of prison. . . . And changed his prison garments: and did eat bread continually before him all the days of his life. And his allowance was a continual allowance given him of the king, a daily rate for every day, all the days of his life." (II Kings 25:27–30) Recently near the Ishtar gate of Babylon some three hundred dated tablets were found. On one of these, dated 592 B.C., there is a record of the rations issued to the prisoners of Babylon, including the name of "Yaukin, king of Judah, and his five sons." The spelling Yaukin for Jehoiachin is the same as that found stamped on jar handles of that day in Palestine, which would seem to make the identification certain. In I Chronicles 3:17, Jehoiachin is said to have had seven sons; a lesser number would be presumed at an earlier date. Here, then, is a dated ration card, so to speak, proving the presence of Jehoiachin in Babylon at the time he is thought to have been there and showing that he did indeed receive a daily ration as the Scriptures relate.

The nearby city fortress of Lachish provides clear proof that it had been twice burned over a short period of time, coinciding with the two captures of Jerusalem. In Lachish the imprint of a clay seal was found, its back still showing the fibers of the papyrus to which it had been attached. It reads: "The property of Gedaliah who is over the house." We meet this distinguished individual in II Kings 25:22, where we are told: "And as for the people that remained in the land of Judah, whom Nebuchadnezzar king of Babylon had left, even over them he made Gedaliah ... ruler." Also found at Lachish, in a room beside the outer gate of the city, were twenty-one ostraca of unusual interest. All had been inscribed just before the fall of the city. These are written in a Hebrew alphabet midway between the earliest alphabetical writing found at Serabit and the later Phoenician alphabet, evidence that the Phoenician Hebrew alphabet was in common use in Palestine at the time of the captivity. Thus the keeping of records was plainly possible—a finding hailed by Dr. Harry T. Torczyner, Bialik Professor of Hebrew at the Hebrew University in Jerusalem, as "the most important discovery of modern times in respect to Biblical criticism." As a result of the captivity, the Phoenician Hebrew script was superseded by the antique Aramaic script, the script used in nearly all the extant copies of the Old Testament in Hebrew. Thus Lachish confirms the Bible story of two conquests of Judah, the presence of Gedaliah as governor and the prevalence of written records before the captivity.

# II

# THE RISE OF
# PERSIA

IT IS NOT UNTIL THE DAYS OF THE CAPTIVITY THAT THE BIBLE REFLECTS the influence of the rising empire of Persia. It seems to have been before 1500 B.C. that the Aryan tribes moved into what is modern Iran, apparently coming in two waves—the Medes, who settled in the northwestern part of present-day Iran, and the Persians, whose capital was fixed in Elam to the southwest. Ecbatana, which almost certainly underlies the modern city of Hamadan, became the Median capital. In the days of Nebuchadnezzar his empire was bounded on the northeast, north and northwest by the Median Empire. Indeed it was a coalition of the Medes and Babylonians that overthrew the ancient Assyrian empire and made possible the glorious advance of Babylon.

It is striking that the rise and victories of Cyrus are repeatedly noted in the Scriptures. Isaiah, chapters 41–43 refers to Cyrus by the amazing titles "Anointed of the Lord," the "Lord's Messiah." Since Cyrus was not a believer in the God of Isaiah, as indeed Isaiah testifies, this is most remarkable. Isaiah speaks of God as saying to Cyrus, "I girded thee, though thou hast not known me," and points to the victories of Cyrus as revealing God's own power. By 549 B.C., Cyrus had moved north, conquered Ecbatana and united the two kingdoms into what thenceforth was known as the land of the Medes and the Persians. Shortly after, by a brilliant winter campaign, he overthrew King Croesus of Lydia, whose wealthy empire included most of modern Turkey. In 539 Cyrus defeated a Chaldean army and entered Babylon. We have a record of this conquest from three different sources, from a record left by Nabonidus, the defeated king of Babylon, from Cyrus' own record and from a brief account in the Book of Daniel.

Nabonidus described his defeat in these words:

In the month of Tashritu, when Cyrus attacked the army of Akkad in Opis on the Tigris, the inhabitants of Akkad revolted but he (*Nabonidus*) massacred the confused inhabitants. The 15th day, Sippar was seized without battle. Nabonidus fled. The 16th day, Gobryas (*Ugbaru*), the governor of Gutium and the army of Cyrus entered Babylon without battle. Afterwards Nabonidus was arrested in Babylon when he returned (there). . . . In the month of Arahshamnu, the 3rd day, Cyrus entered Babylon, green twigs were spread in front of him—the state of "Peace" (*sulmu*) was imposed upon the city. Cyrus sent greetings to all Babylon. Gobryas, his governor, installed (sub-) governors in Babylon.*

Cyrus recorded:

He [Marduk] scanned and looked (through) all the countries, searching for a righteous ruler willing to lead him [i.e., Marduk] (in the annual procession). (Then) he pronounced the name of Cyrus [*Ku-ra-as*], king of Anshan, declared him (lit.: pronounced [his] name) to be(come) the ruler of all the world. He made the Guti country and all the Manda-hordes bow in submission to his [i.e., Cyrus'] feet. And he [Cyrus] did always endeavour to treat according to justice the black-headed whom he [Marduk] has made him conquer. Marduk, the great lord, a protector of his people worshippers, beheld with pleasure his [i.e., Cyrus'] good deeds and his upright mind [lit.: heart] (and therefore) ordered him to march against his city Babylon (Ká·dingir·ra). He made him set out on the road to Babylon going at his side like a real friend. His widespread troops—their number, like that of the water of a river, could not be established—strolled along, their weapons packed away. Without any battle he made him enter his town Babylon (*Su·an·na*), sparing Babylon (*Ká·dingir·ra^{ki}*) any calamity. He delivered into his [i.e., Cyrus'] hands Nabonidus, the king who did not worship him [i.e., Marduk]. All the inhabitants of Babylon as well as of the entire country of Sumer and Akkad, princes and governors (included), bowed to him [Cyrus] and kissed his feet, jubilant that he (had received) the kingship and with shining faces. Happily they greeted him as master through whose help they had come

* Pritchard, *op. cit.*, p. 306.

(again) to life from death (and) had all been spared damage and disaster, and they worshipped his (very) name. . . .

When I entered Babylon as a friend and (when) I established the seat of government in the palace of the ruler under jubilation and rejoicing, Marduk, the great lord, [induced] the magnanimous inhabitants of Babylon [to love me], and I was daily endeavouring to worship him. My numerous troops walked around in Babylon in peace.*

The Biblical account is found in Daniel 5:25–31. There is only a brief account of the fall of the city. Two discrepancies at once arrest our attention. In the Book of Daniel the ruler of Babylon is Belshazzar, not Nabonidus, and the conqueror of the city is designated as Darius the Mede. The Bible contains the dramatic tale of Belshazzar's feast, his impious bringing of the vessels stolen from Jerusalem into his banquet and the mysterious hand that appeared to write on the wall a warning of impending doom. Daniel is called in and interprets the message for the trembling Belshazzar, who makes him the third in the kingdom and places a chain of gold about his neck. It would appear then that Belshazzar, not Nabonidus, was king, but this would contradict what both Nabonidus and Cyrus have recorded. The apparent contradiction has been solved by other inscriptions. In these Belshazzar is named as the first-born son of Nabonidus, who has left this statement:

> He (Nabonidus) entrusted the "Camp" to his oldest (son), the first-born,
> The troops everywhere in the country he ordered under his (command).
> He let (everything) go, entrusted the kingship to him
> And, himself, he started out for a long journey,
> The (military) forces of Akkad marching with him;
> He turned towards Tema (deep) in the west.

Subsequent records coming from the seventh, ninth, tenth, and eleventh years of the reign of Nabonidus note that he was in Arabia and his son in Akkad. Belshazzar, then, had been made king over that region before its fall. This dual kingship also explains why it was not in Belshazzar's power to make Daniel the second in the kingdom as one might have expected. He himself was second, and his father first. Daniel could only be third.

* *Ibid.*, pp. 315-316.

Archeology has as yet thrown no light on who "Darius the Mede" may have been. Some have suggested that Darius may have been another name for Gobryas who first took the city, but as yet there is no evidence to support this assumption. Darius I, grandson of Cyrus, did enter Babylon some time later, in 521 B.C., after the city had revolted.

By the conquest of Babylon Cyrus became master of the political, religious, commercial and cultural center of the world of his day and overthrew the last great Semitic empire. Thereafter the Aryans, represented by the Persians, Greeks and Romans, took over. One of Cyrus' first changes in policy was to reverse the deportation strategy of his predecessors. He records:

(As to the region) from . . . as far as Asshur and Susa, Agade, Eshnunna, the towns Zamban, Me-turnu, Der as well as the region of the Gutians, I returned to (these) sacred cities on the other side of the Tigris, the sanctuaries of which have been ruins for a long time, the images which (used) to live therein and established for them permanent sanctuaries. I (also) gathered all their (former) inhabitants and returned (to them) their habitations. Furthermore, I resettled upon the command of Marduk, the great lord, all the gods of Sumer and Akkad whom Nabonidus has brought into Babylon ($Su\cdot na\cdot na^{ki}$) to the anger of the lord of the gods, unharmed, in their (former) chapels, the places which make them happy.

May all the gods whom I have resettled in their sacred cities ask daily Bel and Nebo for a long life for me and may they recommend me (to him); to Marduk, my lord, they may say this: "Cyrus, the king who worships you, and Cambyses, his son . . ."[*]

It is in full harmony with this recorded policy that Cyrus should permit the Jews to return to their homeland as the prophets had foretold. Their return to that desolate land is recorded in the Book of Ezra, chapters 5, 6. Archeological studies in Palestine have revealed how terribly the land had suffered at the hands of Nebuchadnezzar. Towns and cities everywhere were destroyed and the inhabitants deported. It was centuries before the land returned to its former greatness.

Cyrus was succeeded by his son Cambyses, who died after a reign of only eight years. Then came Darius I, Darius the Great. With his accession, the religion of Zoroaster became the official religion of the empire. It is to this Darius that the Bible refers. As

[*] *Ibid.*, p. 316.

TRIPYLON RELIEF AT PERSEPOLIS, SHOWING KING DARIUS I (SEATED) AND XERXES

recorded in the Book of Haggai, a prophetic message was delivered to Zerubbabel on the first day of the sixth month of the second year of Darius, August 29, 520 B.C. The prophet Zechariah's first sermon was delivered in the eighth month of the same year (or October–November). The completion of the rebuilt temple in Jerusalem is noted as occurring on the third of Adar in the sixth year of Darius, March 12, 515. In Daniel, chapter 6, there is reference to the careful and extensive organization that was a pronounced feature of Darius' reign.

There are three great memorials to Darius the Great in Iran today. The most valuable from the standpoint of archeology is the Besitun inscription. It proved the key that unlocked the secrets of cuneiform writing. The most magnificent memorial to Darius is the vast collection of palaces called Jemshid's Throne by Iranians and Persepolis by others. The third memorial is Darius' huge rock-carved tomb, Naqsh-i Rostam, the carvings of Rostam.

Cyrus first built his capital at Pasargadae, some twenty-five miles from Persepolis, whose ruins are even now being explored. Darius then transferred the capital to Persepolis and proceeded to erect a magnificent group of buildings on a huge artificial platform over fifteen hundred feet long. This remained the Achaemenian spring capital until the empire was overthrown by Alexander the Great. Excavations on this site were conducted by Ernst Herzfeld in 1931–1934 under the sponsorship of the Oriental Institute of the University of Chicago and in 1935–1939 by Erich F. Schmidt. Work goes on under the Iranian Department of Antiquities. A colossal gateway flanked by winged bulls with human heads has been discovered, a great reception hall called the Apadana, its roof supported by seventy-two enormous columns, a hall of one hundred columns even more immense, the harems of Darius and Xerxes and the house of the royal treasury. In this complex of palaces Achaemenian architecture reached its zenith and to the present day has never been equaled in Iran.

Xerxes, the son of Cyrus, so frequently represented in the carvings at Persepolis, is doubtless the Ahasuerus mentioned in Ezra 4:6. His successor Artaxerxes is the king who sent Nehemiah to Jerusalem in his twentieth year. In Ezra 7:1 we read that Ezra came to Jerusalem in the seventh year of Artaxerxes. If this reference is to Artaxerxes I, it would bring Ezra to Jerusalem in 485 B.C., before the arrival of Nehemiah; if the reference is to Artaxerxes II,

AERIAL VIEW OF THE
Persepolis, a magnificent memorial to Darius, was composed
Achaemenian

RUINS OF PERSEPOLIS

of a vast collection of palaces which represented the zenith of
architecture.

then the date would be 398 B.C. The Book of Nehemiah relates how Sanballat of Samaria attempted to frustrate Nehemiah's plans to rebuild Jerusalem. The name of Sanballat is mentioned in the Elephantine papyri, documents written by Egyptian Jews in Aramaic and dated in the fifth century B.C. Sanballat is identified as the father of two men who acted as governors of Samaria in 408 B.C. Another name is that of Johanan, who is described as high priest in Jerusalem at the same time. Johanan was the son of Eliashib (Nehemiah 12:23) and Eliashib was chief priest and helper in the rebuilding of Jerusalem (Nehemiah 3:1). This would accord with the Elephantine papyrus and gives reason to believe that Ezra followed Nehemiah rather than preceded him, as is usually assumed from the order of the books in the Bible.

*Courtesy of the Oriental Institute, University of Chicago*

THE PALACE OF DARIUS AT PERSEPOLIS

# 12

# WRITING
# AND ANCIENT
# MANUSCRIPTS

## *Leading Bible Manuscripts*

ARCHEOLOGICAL INVESTIGATIONS HAVE LED MANY SCHOLARS TO THE conviction that the art of writing stems from southern Mesopotamia among the Sumerians in the prehistoric period. Not only do the earliest forms of writing yet discovered come from the temple yard of ancient Uruk, the Biblical Erech, but the various steps in the development of writing have been traced in the ruins of Mesopotamian cities. A cylindrical seal was first used by the Sumerians to identify persons, cities or gods. It was found that these could be used to make an impression on a clay tablet, and from this beginning picture writing, writing in syllables and writing alphabetically slowly developed.

The materials used for writing varied from country to country and were inevitably influenced by the climate. In Mesopotamia, where the climate is dry and mud abundant, sun-dried or baked tablets were used from the first. The great Ashurbanipal library consisted of some sixty thousand of these tablets. In Iran, where there is more rock and the climate is wetter, many of the most important carvings and inscriptions are on the solid rock and some of the more elegant on tablets of silver and gold. At the same time clay tablets were also used, as is evidenced by the finding of several thousand tablets in the ruins of Persepolis.

In Egypt, where papyrus plants grow along the muddy shore of the Nile, it was discovered that a very lasting form of writing material could be manufactured from these plants. The papyrus grows in shallow water, has a stalk that may become as thick as a man's arm and may be fifteen feet tall. The pith is cut into flat strips and laid side by side. Another layer with the grain running at right angles is laid on top, and the two layers are pasted together. The pieces thus made are then pasted into long strips and the surfaces smoothed. About twenty sheets are combined to make a single roll, which may be from two to fifteen inches high. An average roll may be thirty to thirty-five feet long. One enormous roll, on which were written the Chronicles of King Ramses II, was some one hundred and thirty-three feet long and seventeen inches high. Usually the rolls were written on only one side, the writing running parallel to the grain of the papyrus, but some rolls have been found with writing on both sides. In Revelation 5:1, for example, such a papyrus roll is mentioned; many have been found. The pen used by the scribes was a dried split reed. There were two common forms of ink, one made of lampblack, gum and water and another of nut-galls, green vitriol and water. In the first century a scroll, called a *biblion*, was commonly used; the plural is *biblia*. It is from the latter that we get our word Bible, meaning "scrolls," although the Greek word for scroll in turn was originally taken from the word *biblos*, meaning pith, the inner part of the papyrus plant.

In Palestine a common writing material was a tablet of wood coated with wax, usually black in color, on which writing was scratched with a stylus. It is this to which reference is made in Luke 1:63. Such records were, of course, temporary; the writing could be removed by melting the wax. Schoolboys carried such tablets, called caudex, fastened at their waists. Often two tablets were carried; a raised edge kept them from rubbing together and protected the writing. From the caudex, the codex or booklike form of manuscript was developed. Oblong pieces of papyrus were sewn together along one edge. The advantage of this form was that one could turn immediately to the middle or to the end of such a book, whereas a scroll had to be unrolled. It is possible but by no means certain that the codex was developed by the early Christians. At any rate they were among the earliest to adopt it and habitually used the codex long before the pagans gave up scrolls.

In Palestine the people often used ostraca, broken pieces of pottery, as a means of simple record. Thousands have been found bearing such items as notes, receipts, school exercises and records; many bear one or two verses of the New Testament. It has been suggested that these may well have served as amulets. Some of the most interesting finds at Lachish were written on such ostraca.

Papyrus was not so much used in Palestine because it had to be imported and because in the damper climate it was apt to rot. In early days leather and refinements of leather—parchment made from sheepskin and vellum made from lambskin—came into general use for more valuable documents. The prophecy of Jeremiah which, as we read in Jeremiah 36:23, the king slashed to pieces with a knife and threw into the fire, was probably written on leather. In the second letter to Timothy Paul asks that certain parchments be sent to him—probably vellum rolls of Old Testament books (Timothy 4:13). By the fourth century vellum had superseded papyrus throughout most of the Roman Empire. In 332, the Emperor Constantine instructed Eusebius to have prepared for the churches in the new capital of his empire fifty vellum copies of the Bible. They were written in threefold and fourfold, that is, with three or four columns to the page, and bound in such a way that the flesh side of a vellum sheet faced the flesh side of another, the hair side another hair side. Lines drawn on the hair side were heavy enough to show through the sheet and serve as guides in writing on the reverse.

The oldest style of Greek writing is called *uncial*. The word may refer to the fact that a letter occupies one twelfth of a line, as is sometimes the case. Some scholars point out that uncial can also mean inch and may refer to the height of the letters, which might, with some exaggeration, be called inch-high; or, with more exaggeration, inch-broad. All of the oldest New Testament codices, from the fourth to the ninth centuries, were written in uncials. Later, small connected letters known as minuscules were introduced, and this change provides one means of rough approximation in the dating of old manuscripts. Another aid to positive dating is the introduction of punctuation. The earliest manuscripts are unpunctuated; words were strung together without separation. The gradual introduction of punctuation marks, by no means systematically, is studied as an aid in estimating the age of manuscripts, as are the separation of words and the beginning of paragraphing. The earliest manuscripts divided the Gospel into sections, without chapter divisions. In 1238, under the direction of Cardinal Hugo de S Caro, the first copies of the Bible divided by chapters were made. The division of chapters into verses was the work of one Robert Etienne, about 1551.

## LEADING BIBLE MANUSCRIPTS

Of the literally thousands of manuscripts bearing portions or fragments of the Bible, four are recognized as being the most complete and the most valuable. Of these the finest and probably the oldest is the Codex Vaticanus, so called because it was originally a treasure of the Vatican library in Rome and has been safeguarded there for most of its recorded history. Its name and description are in the first catalogue of the Vatican library, compiled in 1475. After the conquest of Italy, Napoleon carried the manuscript off to Paris where it remained from 1809 to 1815. While there it was studied by a Catholic scholar from Tübingen and its antiquity and value were recognized. In the years 1889–1890 the entire manuscript was photographed, page by page, and copies were offered for sale to universities and museums. The manuscript was originally of 820 leaves, of which 759 are once again in the Vatican library. The unpunctuated manuscript is written with three columns and forty-two lines to the page. Experts believe it was transcribed early in the fourth century, some time between A.D. 325–350.

The second most famous manuscript is called the Codex Sinaiticus, so called because it was found at Mount Sinai. Near the foot of the mountain, reputed to be the Sinai mentioned in the Old Testament, there has been a monastery since the fourth century. It was ordered built by Queen Helena, the mother of Constantine, about A.D. 327, and it is claimed to enclose the site of the burning bush which Moses saw. The monastery of St. Catherine is named for the lady Catherine martyred under the Emperor Maximian (A.D. 305–313). Built as a fort high above the plain, its isolation has enabled the monastery to escape destruction for over fifteen hundred years.

The discoverer of the Codex Sinaiticus was Dr. Constantin von Tischendorf, a German scholar, who upon hearing in 1844 that the monastery housed some very old manuscripts set out to visit the remote spot. Almost at once he noticed in the hall a large basket containing some old parchments. He was told that these were to be burned, and that two such basket loads had already been burned. He asked to be allowed to examine the manuscripts and was permitted to do so. Dr. Tischendorf spent most of the night studying what he recognized as being a marvelous treasure. There were forty-five sheets in this copy of the Bible, and he was allowed to take them with him for further study. In 1853 and again in 1859 he returned to Sinai, hoping to find additional pages. The night before he was to depart after his second visit, one of the monks brought him a large bundle wrapped in cloth. To his delight he found it to be what he was seeking. The bundle contained pages representing a large part of the Old Testament and all of the New and, in addition, the so-called Epistle of Barnabas and the Shepherd of Hermas. After considerable negotiations, Dr. Tischendorf was able to have the manuscript transferred to Petrograd on payment of $6,750 to the monastery for its prize. At Petrograd a facsimile was prepared and some time later it was photographed. Following the Russian revolution, the communist government, needing foreign exchange credits and having little or no interest in religious texts, offered the book for sale. Half the price was raised by popular subscription in Great Britain and half provided by the British Museum; the unprecedented amount of £100,000, then equal to half a million dollars, was raised. It is estimated that originally the manuscript contained some 730 pages, of which 390 were recovered, and was written four columns to the page, without separation of words and without punctuation. It is generally believed to have been transcribed about the same time as the Vatican manuscript, although some experts have theorized that it may have been written as late as the sixth century A.D. It is thought by some to be one of fifty copies ordered prepared by the Emperor Constantine.

Not quite so old as the two above, and the second ancient manuscript in point of time to become known, is the Codex Alexandrinus. It was presented to Sir Thomas Roe, the British ambassador to Turkey, in 1624 by one Cyril Lucar, the patriarch of Constantinople. It was claimed to have been written by Thecla, a contemporary of the Apostle Paul, but there is no means by which this can be verified. It seems probable that Cyril brought the manuscript with him from Alexandria where he was patriarch before coming to Constantinople, for there is a note appended which reads: "Made an inalienable gift to the patriarchal cell in the city of Alexandria.

MONASTERY OF

The oldest religious sanctuary in the world. The
the lady Catherine martyred

ST. CATHERINE

monastery, at the foot of Mount Sinai, was named for
under Maximian, A.D. 305-313.

Whosoever shall remove it shall be accursed and cut off. Athanasius the Humble." Athanasius is presumably that patriarch of Alexandria who died in 1308. Of perhaps 820 pages originally, 773 pages are now extant. It contains two columns to the page, with little ornament, and appears to date from the fifth century.

The fourth most famous manuscript is the Codex Ephraem Rescriptus, also dating from the fifth century. As the word *rescriptus* indicates, it is a palimpsest, a manuscript which, when an ancient writing had faded, was used a second time. The original manuscript of the Old and New Testaments had faded out by the twelfth century; the parchment was then used for writing the discourses of a fourth-century theologian known as Ephraem Syrus. The manuscript was for many years in the possession of the Medicis in Florence and was brought to Paris in the sixteenth century by Catherine de Medici, who became the wife of Henry II of France. It was recognized that the original writing was of a Biblical nature, but no one succeeded in reading the manuscript until Tischendorf studied it in 1842 and published the results the following year. He found that 145 of the total number of 209 pages were of the New Testament, in one column, without separation between words.

Thus it will be seen that the best ancient manuscripts of the Bible were unknown or unrecognized at the time of the famous King James translation in 1611. For this reason later scholars have found new revisions of that translation necessary. Paradoxical as it may sound, the latest translation of the Bible represents a much earlier version than that of 1611 because it is based on earlier manuscripts.

In addition to the above manuscripts of first importance, hundreds of other manuscripts and fragments of the Bible have been found. There are today over 170 papyrus manuscripts and fragments, over 200 uncial manuscripts and over 2,400 miniscules. Inevitably the copyists who transcribed these manuscripts made mistakes, and these mistakes have been copied, so that variations in the texts amount to thousands in the aggregate. Most of these variant readings are insignificant and easily recognized. It is estimated that there are substantial variations for only about one thousandth of the text as a whole. Of other Greco-Roman writings of the first and second centuries, there is, ordinarily, only one manuscript, and we are forced to depend on copies made much later. We have infinitely more accurate and certainly many more manuscripts of the Bible than of any other ancient book.

# 13

# A CENTURY OF
# DISCOVERY

THE LAST HUNDRED YEARS HAVE BROUGHT THE DISCOVERY OF THOU-
sands of documents buried in the sands of Egypt. Some have been
of the Bible, or portions of it, and many more are documents of all
sorts illuminating our understanding of the life and times of the
first centuries. Only recently have scholars come to realize the
value of these papyrus fragments scattered throughout the dry
sands of Egypt. In 1778 a European dealer purchased a papyrus
manuscript from an Egyptian peasant, who told him he had already
burned fifty such manuscripts for their aromatic odor.

During the nineteenth century the fellahin of Egypt learned that
there were purchasers for manuscripts and began to bring them to
the cities for sale. Archeologists realized that here was a practically inexhaustible storehouse of manuscripts concerned with
ancient Egypt.

In 1877 a great mass of papyri was found buried near the ancient
city of Arsinoe, or Crocodilopolis, in Fayum Egypt. The city, about
eighty miles south of Cairo, is near an oasis and at one time had
been the center of the worship of the crocodile. Just south of the
oasis is the site of the ancient city of Oxyrhynchus which in the
fourth and fifth centuries (A.D.) had been an important Christian
stronghold with many churches and monasteries. Systematic diggings at both these sites uncovered the old city refuse mounds
where an infinite variety of scraps of papyrus had been dumped.
In the old cemetery Dr. Flinders Petrie unearthed a quantity of
papyri used to make the inner linings of coffins. They were recovered and read. One of the richest stores of papyri was discovered
as a result of a worker's exasperation. Digging, he came across a

crocodile cemetery. His spade uncovered one mummified crocodile after another. In his anger he threw one of the mummies violently to the ground. It burst open, revealing that the crocodile had been wrapped in papyri. Other crocodiles were discovered to have been stuffed with papyri. From this unexpected source a considerable addition was made to the quantity of ancient writings available for study.

It was at Oxyrhynchus that two leaves of papyri were found bearing lists of the sayings of Jesus, most of which differ to some extent from those recorded in the New Testament.

"And then shalt thou see clearly to cast out the mote that is in thy brother's eye." The similarity to Matthew 7:5 is striking.

"Except ye keep [your life in] the world as a fast, ye shall not find the Kingdom of God; except ye keep the [whole] week as a sabbath, ye shall not see the Father." This saying seems in the spirit of Jesus as revealed in the Gospel and is quite possibly authentic.

"Jesus saith, I stood in the midst of the world, and in the flesh was I seen of them, and I found all men drunken, and none found I athirst among them, and my soul grieveth over the sons of men, because they are blind in their heart, poor and know not their poverty." Echoes of Gospel teaching will be noted.

"Jesus saith, wherever there are two they are not without God, and if one is alone anywhere, I say I am with him. Raise the stone, there shalt thou find me, cleave the wood, and I am there." This may be compared with Matthew 18:20.

It was the discovery of the Oxyrhynchus manuscript which inspired Henry Van Dyke's "The Toiling of Felix":

> Hear a word that Jesus spake
>   Eighteen centuries ago,
> Where the crimson lilies blow
>   Round the blue Tiberian lake:
> There the bread of life he brake,
>   Through the fields of harvest walking
>   With his lowly comrades, talking
> Of the secret thoughts that feed
> Weary hearts in time of need.
>   Art thou hungry? Come and take;
>   Hear the word that Jesus spake:

'Tis the sacrament of labour; meat and drink divinely blest;
Friendship's food, and sweet refreshment; strength and courage,
  joy and rest.

.     .     .     .     .     .     .     .     .     .     .

Hear the Master's risen word!
  Delving spades have set it free,—
  Wake! the world has need of thee,—
Rise, and let thy voice be heard,
Like a fountain disinterred.
  Upward springing, singing, sparkling;
  Through the doubtful shadows darkling;
Till the clouds of pain and rage
Brooding o'er the toiling age,
  As with rifts of light are stirred
  By the music of the Word;
Gospel for the heavy-laden, answer to the
  labourer's cry;
*"Raise the stone, and thou shalt find Me; cleave
  the wood, and there am I."**

"Jesus saith, a prophet is not acceptable in his own country,
neither doth a physician work cures upon them that know him."
The first part of this is akin to Luke 4:24; the second part seems an
echo of Luke 4:23, but the meaning is quite different.

"Jesus saith, a City built on the top of a high hill and firmly established can neither fall nor be hid." Recalling Matthew 5:14.

"Jesus saith, Thou hearest with one ear, [but the other ear thou
hast closed]."† This is not echoed in the Gospels but seems to refer
to those who listen to what they desire to hear of the promises of
God but are deaf to their obligations.

The second papyrus, found at Oxyrhynchus in 1904, begins in this
way: "These are the [wonderful] words which Jesus the living Lord
spake [to the disciples] and to Thomas, and he said to them: Every
one that hearkens to these words shall never taste death."‡ (The
words in brackets are supplied as being necessary to the meaning.)
Then follow several somewhat longer sayings; the first is: "Jesus

* Henry Van Dyke, *The Toiling of Felix and Other Poems* (New York: Charles
Scribner's Sons, 1900), pp. 3-5.
† Quoted in Finegan, *op. cit.*, p. 323.
‡ G. A. Barton, *Archaeology and the Bible* (Philadelphia: Sunday-School Union,
1916), p. 430.

saith, Let not him who seeks . . . cease until he finds, and when he finds he shall be astonished; astonished he shall reach the kingdom, and having reached the kingdom he shall rest." This resembles Gospel verses at several points. The second reads: "Jesus saith, [Ye ask who are those] that draw us [to the kingdom, if] the kingdom is in heaven? . . . the fowls of the air, and all the beasts that are under the earth or upon the earth, and the fishes of the sea, [these are they which draw] you, and the kingdom of heaven is within you; and whosoever shall know himself shall find it. [Strive therefore] to know yourselves, and ye shall be aware that ye are the sons of the [Almighty] Father [and] ye shall be aware that ye are in [the city of God] and ye are [the city.]" Aside from the thought "the kingdom of heaven is within you" none of this is found in the Gospels.*

Another saying: "Jesus saith, A man shall not hesitate . . . to ask . . . concerning his place [in the kingdom. Ye shall know] that many that are first shall be last and the last first. . . ." Another: "Jesus saith, Everything that is not before thy face and that which is hidden from thee shall be revealed to thee. For there is nothing hidden which shall not be made manifest, nor buried which shall not be raised."† The last sentence parallels Matthew 10:26. A final saying is too broken to be intelligible.

We may never know whether the above sayings are rightfully identified as the sayings of Jesus, although it is probable that some of them are. The Gospel of Luke says that many before have written of Jesus, and in the Book of John it is said that the world itself would not have space for all the books that might be written about the life of Jesus. We can be sure that much that Jesus said and did was not recorded and that many of his sayings do not appear in the Four Gospels.

Other letters and notes have been found which throw light on the moral and spiritual life of ancient days. One such, a letter with a date that corresponds to 1 B.C., was written by a somewhat illiterate man to a lady whom he calls his sister, probably meaning his wife. "Hilarion to Alis his sister, heartiest greetings. . . . Know that we are still even now in Alexandria. . . . I beg and beseech of you to take care of the little child. And as soon as we receive wages I will send them to you. If—good luck to you!—you bear a child,

* *Ibid.*
† *Ibid.*, p. 431.

if it is a boy, let it live; if it is a girl, expose it. You told Aphrodisias, 'Do not forget me.' How can I forget you? I beg you, therefore, not to worry."* The writer obviously cares for his wife and is anxious to provide for her. Yet in the most casual way he directs her to allow their baby to die if it is a girl, a common practice in those days. Just at that time another baby, born in Bethlehem, was growing up, perhaps in Egypt, whose life and teachings were destined to change all that.

Another moving letter has been found which might have well been writen by the prodigal son in the parable (Luke 15:11–32). It reads:

Antonis Longus to Nilus his mother, many greetings. Continually I pray for your health. Supplication I direct each day to the lord Serapis (an Egyptian deity). I wish you to know that I had no hope that you would come up to the metropolis. On this account neither did I enter into the city. But I was ashamed to come to Karanis (a village in Egypt, probably his home) because I am going about in rags. I write to you that I am naked. I beseech you, mother, be reconciled to me. But I know what I have brought upon myself. Punished I have been in every way. I know that I have sinned. I hear from Postumus who meet you . . . and unseasonably related all to you. Do you not know that I would rather be a cripple than be conscious that I am still owing you an obol . . . come yourself . . . I have heard that . . . I beseech you . . . I almost . . . I beseech you . . . I will not do otherwise.

Many longer letters have been found. It has been observed that the general outline of these letters is strikingly similar to those written by St. Paul. They include a formal greeting, a thanksgiving, a prayer, the special message of the letter, closing salutation and a valediction. So in form Paul used the style of his day. The expressions "I wish you to know" and "I beseech you," used in the letter given above, are found in the Epistles of St. Paul. But oh, how different the contents of his letters!

One of the most important discoveries to emerge from these fragments and letters is in the matter of the language in which they are written; it is similar to that in which the New Testament is written. Scholars were aware that New Testament Greek differed from classical Greek; indeed, it was like no other Greek whatsoever. It was long considered a special vehicle of inspiration and by some

* Quoted in Finegan, *op. cit.*, pp. 325-326.

was called the "language of the Holy Spirit." But Dr. Adolf Deissman examined the papyri and concluded that it resembled the
common language of Greek-speaking peoples all around the eastern Mediterranean; the disciples had put their message into the
everyday language of the people. Before Dr. Deissman's discovery,
some five hundred of the five thousand words used in the New
Testament were unknown and their meanings had to be worked
out from the context in which they appeared. These unique words
were recognized in other papyri, and in this way both the meaning
and connotation of the New Testament became much more definite.

# 14

# NEWLY
# RECOVERED
# MANUSCRIPTS

ONE OF THE SMALLEST AND ONE OF THE MOST IMPORTANT FRAGMENTS found in recent years is the so-called Rylands manuscript. It contains a very few words, but for two reasons it is vastly important. It is the oldest portion of the New Testament yet found; it is believed to date from about the year A.D. 125. Secondly, although the scrap was found in Egypt it has been identified as a portion of the Gospel of John. In past years there has been much debate about the Book of John. The earliest church traditions say that it was written just before his death. But many Bible scholars believed that it was written at a much later time; some placed it as late as the third century. To find that it was in existence before A.D. 125, and long enough before so that a copy of it had reached Egypt, completely disproves the theory of a later date of composition.

The most important New Testament manuscripts so far discovered are the so-called Chester Beatty papyri. In about 1931 the papyri in question began reaching the bazaars of Cairo and were bought by Chester Beatty of London and by the University of Michigan. They consist of eleven codices containing portions of nine Old Testament books and of fifteen New Testament books, viz., the Four Gospels, the Book of Acts, the Pauline Epistles and the Book of Revelation. The segment containing the letters of Paul comes from about the year A.D. 200. Since Paul wrote his letters to the churches he had founded between A.D. 50 and 60, and the oldest previous manuscript, the Codex Vaticanus, was transcribed some three hundred years later, the discovery of the Beatty papyri cuts in half the time between the actual writing of Paul's letters and the hitherto oldest manuscript copy extant. With two exceptions, Paul's letters from Romans to I Thessalonians appear in the same order as they are presented in the New Testament. Hebrews is inserted between Romans and I Corinthians, and the order of Galatians and Ephesians is reversed. A comparison of the text of these copies of Paul's epistles with the latest translations is remarkable chiefly for the lack of significant change or difference, truly convincing evidence of the care with which the New Testament has been copied and handed down to us.

Another and more recent find, made at the convent of St. Catherine on Mount Sinai, is a copy of the Gospels in Syriac. The manuscript itself was written in the fifth and seventh centuries after Christ and is a copy of a translation of the Gospels which was done in the second century. For this reason it represents an old and independent witness to the original Gospels. The manuscript is a palimpsest, i.e., one bearing two different texts. The earlier is of the Four Gospels, the later is a book of the lives of female saints. When discovered, the leaves were stuck together and it was necessary to steam them apart and treat the manuscript chemically to bring out the older original writing. It contains all but eight pages of the Four Gospels.

Although it is not, in fact, a Gospel manuscript, the discovery in 1881 of the book called the Diatesseron is of high importance. The book was prepared some time during the second century by a Christian convert named Tatian, a member of the Syriac-speaking church in upper Mesopotamia. In it the Four Gospels are woven into one, using all of the material but omitting the repetitions. The work became so popular that it was finally forbidden by the early church out of a fear that the Four Gospels would be neglected. Many references to the Diatesseron were found in early writings, but some scholars believed it could not exist because the proposed compiler Tatian died A.D. 170 and it was thought that the Gospel of John had been written at a later date and thus could not have been a source for the writings of Tatian. It is of considerable significance that several versions of the Diatesseron have turned up in recent years. A page of the Greek version was found in the ancient city of Dura on the Euphrates, where it must have been buried somewhere between 254 and 257, about the time the city was destroyed. Another copy, in Arabic, was found in the Vatican library;

MOUNTAIN OF THE TEN COMMANDMENTS

Mount Moses shown here is commonly accepted as Mount Sinai where
more than three thousand years ago Moses received the Ten Commandments. The monastery of St. Catherine may be seen
in the foreground.

136 PROPHETS, IDOLS AND DIGGERS

later, a Persian translation, made in the thirteenth century, came to light. The Persian copy has recently been published by the Inter-church Literature Committee. Professors at the universities of Teh-ran and Tabriz make use of it in their classes in Persian literature as an excellent example of thirteenth-century Persian. The finding of these copies has settled all doubts as to the existence of this work and as to whether it did include the Gospel of John, as indeed it does. John's Gospel appears in the first chapter.

In addition to Tatian's Diatesseron, a fragment of another, sim-ilar work was discovered in the British Museum and edited by Bell and Skeat in 1935. It seems evident that this work preceded that of Tatian. The unknown author made much freer use of his sources. Probably the manuscript dates from early in the second century. It includes sections of the Gospel of John, thus pushing back still further the date of the composition of the Book of John.

Other archeological finds have served to support the accuracy of John's Gospel and to provide refutation to objections raised by critics. For example, John's use of the Greek word *didaskalos* for teacher was considered anachronistic; it was claimed this was a second-century word not used in the time of Jesus. But the Hebrew scholar Dr. E. L. Sukenik, who made a careful study of ossuaries or burial urns dating before the destruction of Jerusalem A.D. 70, reported finding the word *didaskalos* inscribed on one such ossuary. Other scholars claimed that the proper names used in John are not names current in Palestine in the time of Jesus. Here again, ossuar-ies have provided a convincing rejoinder. The names Miriam, Mar-tha, Elizabeth, Salome, Johanna, Jesus, Joseph and Lazarus have all been found on burial urns, thus proving these names in common use in that day.

Until a few years ago there was no trace in Jerusalem of a pave-ment corresponding to that mentioned in the Book of John, Chapter 19: Pilate "sat down in the judgment seat in a place that is called the Pavement, but in the Hebrew, Gabbatha." Father H. Vincent, the renowned archeologist, excavated a magnificent pavement be-low the so-called *ecce homo* arch and found beside the Tower of Antonia an area of about twenty-five hundred square meters ap-parently serving as a court to that tower. It was a raised, rocky ele-vation; the name Gabbatha (meaning ridge or elevation) was quite proper to such a pavement.

Archeologists have solved the scholar's perplexity about the lo-

JACOB'S WELL

The well was located on the parcel of land purchased by Jacob "for a hundred lambs." Here Joseph's brothers sold him into slavery, and here Christ talked to the Samaritan woman.

cation of the Pool of Bethesda mentioned in the Book of John, Chapter 5. Two particular difficulties existed in placing it: there was no trace of any large pool in ancient Jerusalem; secondly, in the Near East pools are, by tradition, either round or square. But in the Book of John it is specified that the Pool of Bethesda was five-sided and with five porches or porticoes surrounding it. However, some forty years ago, digging began near an old church in Jerusalem; it was reputed to have been built on the site of the Pool of Bethesda. Thirty feet below the present surface was discovered the corner of what had been a very large and deep pool, about forty meters square. It was thus demonstrated that, in fact, there had been a large pool, as reported in the Book of John, but it left unsolved the problem of the five porticoes. Further exploration revealed an adjacent pool of the same size, separated from the first by a broad causeway. It was, then, a double pool, divided by a causeway. With four porticoes, one to a side, and a portico spanning the causeway in the middle, there was place and need for the five porticoes mentioned in the Gospel.

Other sites, such as Jacob's well, Salim and Shechem, near the present city of Noblus, have been identified and found to match references in the Gospel of John. Ancient Hebrew customs, feasts, politics and organizations which came to an end when Jerusalem was destroyed A.D. 70 are all reported with accuracy in the Gospel, as subsequent investigation has proved; for this reason Bible scholars are convinced that the Gospel of John must have been the work of someone who lived in the Jerusalem of that time. It has been claimed that of the Four Gospels, the Book of John may have been the earliest of all.

# 15

# THE DEAD SEA SCROLLS

A WELL-NIGH INCREDIBLE SERIES OF DISCOVERIES, BY FAR THE MOST important finds in Biblical archeology in the twentieth century, began when an Arab boy, searching for a lost goat, found a cave high on a hillside west of the Dead Sea. He threw a stone into the cave and, hearing a crash, entered and found a quantity of broken jars. In some of these were carefully wrapped leather manuscripts of great antiquity. He took the manuscripts to Jerusalem and sold five of them to the metropolitan (bishop) of the Syrian Jacobite church, Mar Athanasius by name, who was head of the monastery of St. Mark. The bishop was unable to read them but he bought them nonetheless, paying a price reputed to be $150, on the chance that they might be of value.

Shortly after, three other manuscripts found at the same place were bought by Dr. E. L. Sukenik, then the head archeologist of the Hebrew University in Jerusalem. He at once realized their great antiquity and noted in his diary "Today I have been shown a piece of a scroll. I do not dare write what I think of it." About this time the Israeli-Arab dispute grew in violence, and the investigations of Mar Athanasius and of Dr. Sukenik were carried out quite independently, neither knowing that the other had obtained some of the Dead Sea scrolls.

Upon being assured that his scrolls were of no great importance, Mar Athanasius got in touch with the American School of Oriental Research. An American archeologist, Dr. John C. Trever, identified the largest of the manuscripts as being a complete copy of the

book of Isaiah, written in a script unlike that of other Hebrew
Bible manuscripts and almost certainly very old. Trever secured
permission to photograph the scroll, a procedure that proved very
difficult because of the shortage of photographic supplies and the
state of war between Arabs and Jews. Eventually Dr. Trever succeeded in photographing the entire manuscript. Some of the photo-
graphs were sent to Dr. William Foxwell Albright of Johns Hopkins University, Director of the American School of Oriental Research in Jerusalem, perhaps the leading authority on the subject.
From Albright, he received the following reply: "My heartiest con-
gratulations on the greatest manuscript discovery of modern times."
Albright thought the Isaiah scroll should be dated around 100 B.C.
and was sure there could be not the slightest doubt of its genuine-
ness. Soon after the discovery was announced, Dr. Sukenik announced his own acquisitions, of a somewhat later date. When we
consider that, until this time, the oldest Bible manuscript in Hebrew came from the tenth century A.D., we can appreciate what a
thrilling and sensational event it was to find a Hebrew manuscript
bridging more than half the time between the writing of Isaiah
and the oldest manuscript previously known.

The ancient date was not immediately accepted; indeed, it was
violently opposed by many scholars. There broke out what has been
amusingly termed "the battle of the scrolls." Some scholars were
for placing a medieval date on the manuscripts, and the proponents
of the early date were required to give irrefutable evidence to support their conviction. Evidence was sought along three lines, the
archeologic, the paleographic and by means of the carbon-14 test.
As soon as conditions permitted, archeologists went down to the
Dead Sea and excavated the floor of the cave where the manuscripts had been found. Bits of pottery and other artifacts indicated
that the cave had been used as a storeroom in the first century A.D.
Later, a nearby ruin was excavated and proved to be a monastery
occupied by those who had transcribed the manuscripts. Coins
found in the ruined monastery proved beyond question that the
site was occupied during the first century B.C. and the early part of
the first century A.D.

Careful study of the handwriting on these and other documents
taken from the cave aided in determining proper dates for the manuscripts by reconstructing the changes in the way various letters
were written over several centuries. Ultimately tens of thousands

of manuscript fragments were found. Study continues. Enough has been read to support Dr. Albright's date in the first century B.C. In this manner the second link in the chain of evidence was forged.

The third link was provided by the delicate carbon-14 test described in the Introduction. Some of the linen cloth in which the manuscripts were wrapped was sent to the University of Chicago for testing. The report on the age of the linen gave a date of A.D. 37, plus or minus two hundred years. There seems no longer any reasonable doubt that the manuscripts were stored around A.D. 70 and that some were very old at the time they were placed in the jars.

The first finds included two Isaiah manuscripts, a commentary on Habakkuk, a book of thanksgiving psalms, a Manual of Discipline, a book called "The War of the Sons of Light and the Sons of Darkness" and a book once thought to be a copy of the lost Book of Lamech, but which has proved to be a commentary on a portion of Genesis. Of these, the Isaiah manuscript bought by Mar Athanasius is the most complete. It was written on seventeen sheets of leather and the leather sheets were sewn together; the sheets varied from fifteen to twenty-five inches in width and were about ten and one-half inches high, making a scroll some twenty-four feet long. Stains on the back of the scroll show that it was in use for a considerable time before being stored away, as does the fact that in one place it had been torn and mended. There are many variations in spelling and grammatical structure, but the contents of the scroll and of the tenth-century manuscript are substantially the same, a remarkable witness to the fidelity of the copyists. Fortunately, the Isaiah manuscript was discovered in time to be consulted in the making of the new Revised Version of the Bible in English; there were only three places where the Dead Sea manuscript determined a change, and nine places where marginal notes in the Revised Version refer to its reading.

The Habakkuk commentary, dating from the first century B.C., has precipitated another wordy argument among Old Testament scholars. The commentary attempts to explain the Book of Habakkuk in the light of contemporary events, indicating certain foreign invaders as the Kittim people. Unfortunately, this does not enlighten us today; no one is certain who the Kittim were—some think they were Romans, others, the Macedonians or the Greeks. The debate continues.

The Manual of Discipline, in two scrolls, is a series of detailed,

THE ISAIAH

One of the most important manuscript discoveries ever made. This and
tests and other archeological evidence

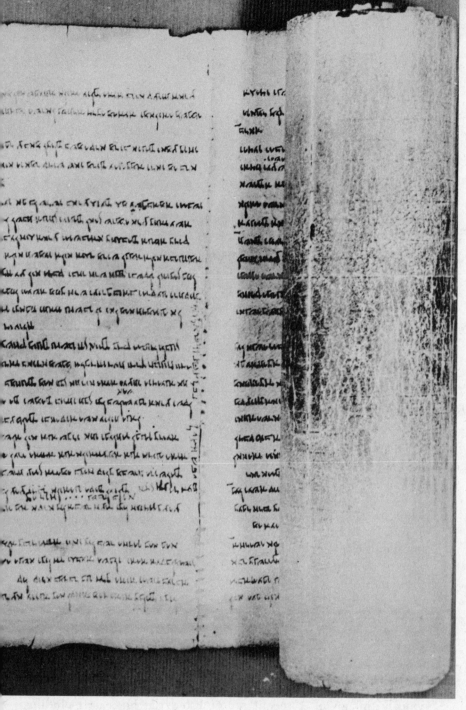

SCROLL

other scrolls found close to the Dead Sea were proved by intricate
to date from the first century or earlier.

rigorous rules of conduct for persons belonging to a religious order, now generally agreed to be that of the Essenes.

Among Dr. Sukenik's manuscripts is one called "The War of the Sons of Light and the Sons of Darkness." This too is an obscure work, and it is not agreed whether it should be interpreted as fiction or fact, history or prophecy. In addition, Sukenik found he had bought a second Isaiah manuscript, but one that should be dated about two hundred years later than the bishop's manuscript. Another of the Sukenik manuscripts is a collection of thanksgiving psalms, in many respects similar to our Book of Psalms.

The last of these amazing finds to be deciphered was a book so tightly wrapped and so rotted by time that at first scholars despaired of being able to open and read it. The name Lamech on a scrap torn from the scroll made it seem possible that this might be a copy of the Book of Lamech, one of the lost Apocrypha. It was opened with the utmost care and discovered to be a lively commentary on portions of the Book of Genesis. The first portion is badly crumpled and in a fragmentary state. It begins with Chapter 5 and follows the general outline of the story of Noah as related in the Book of Enoch. A section in a better state of preservation covers Genesis, chapters 12, 13, 14 and a part of 15, and contains an impressive description of the beauty of Sarah, the wife of Abraham and the mother of Isaac.

Spurred on by these exciting discoveries, archeologists and Bedouins commenced a fevered treasure hunt among the thousands of Judean caves in the vicinity, entering hundreds of caves and finding manuscripts or portions of manuscripts in no less than thirty-nine of them. Cave No. 4 proved especially rich, yielding tens of thousands of manuscript fragments; it is considered to be an even more valuable discovery than the first cave. Some twelve miles away, in a valley called Wady Murabba'at, another large collection of manuscripts dating from the first and second centuries A.D. was discovered. Fragments from about five hundred different manuscripts have been found, representing every Book in the Old Testament except the Book of Esther and many other writings previously unknown. A recent report listed the finds as including, among others, at least some portions of ten copies of Genesis, ten of Exodus, eight of Leviticus, seven of Numbers, seventeen or eighteen of Deuteronomy, two of Joshua, three of Judges, fifteen of Psalms, four of Jeremiah, six of Daniel and eight of the minor prophets. There are so many that some scholars predict that it will take fifty years to read them all.

It is impossible to discuss here all that has been found, but some items are of outstanding interest. One consists of some fragments of a manuscript of the Book of Leviticus and is thought to be from the late fourth century B.C. or early in the third century; if so, it would be the very oldest piece of the Bible yet found. Another find in cave No. 2 was two tightly rolled copper scrolls, badly oxidized and far too fragile to unroll. It was evident that they bore writing on the inside and just enough could be deciphered to make them most tantalizing. Eventually Dr. Baker of Manchester University succeeded in cutting the rolls into strips. He used a tiny saw wheel and worked with such care that he did not destroy a single letter. When translated the scrolls were found to record the location of a vast hoard of gold and silver, to a weight of some two hundred tons. The treasure is believed to have been buried in a wide area about Jerusalem but the exact locations are difficult for searchers to identify. The puzzle of the contents of the copper scrolls has given way to the mystery of the locations of the buried treasure, a treasure that would make Captain Kidd's wealth seem like so much small change! But whether this treasure exists we cannot tell.

From the viewpoint of the Biblical archeologist, another significant find is that of a fragment of a copy of the Book of Ecclesiastes dating from about 150 B.C. Some critics contend that the Book of Ecclesiastes reflects a very "late" point of view and were inclined to date its composition as from the first century or even the second century A.D. But this find, indicating that it was in circulation as early as 150 B.C., disproves the theory of later composition.

Interesting variants in Biblical texts have appeared, some of which are almost certainly authentic and accurate copies of the original. One of these, to be interpolated in I Samuel, would have it that Hannah as she presented her infant son to Eli said: "I will present him a Nazarite forever." In the Septuagint, the Greek version of the Old Testament, Samuel is referred to as a Nazarite.

For the determination of the text of the Old Testament, the most surprising development has been the realization that these hundreds of Hebrew manuscripts reveal three "families" of texts so to speak, three divergent lines in the original Hebrew. It was well known that there are many differences between the Septuagint

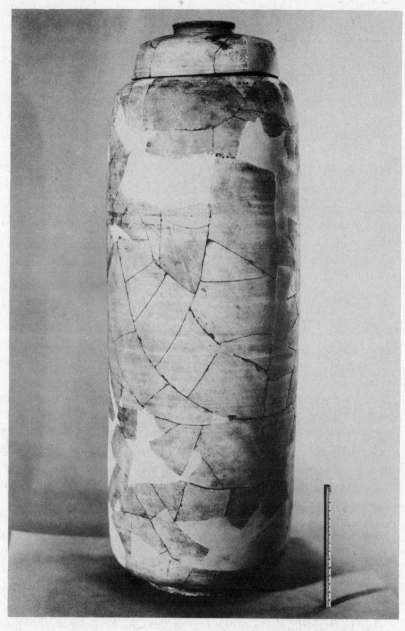

A SCROLL JAR

One of the jars in which were stored the precious manuscripts found
near the Dead Sea.

translation of the Old Testament, made around 250 B.C., and the accepted Hebrew text we now use, but it was supposed that divergences represented careless or inexact translations. Now it is evident that the Septuagint is an accurate translation of one "family" of the early Hebrew text and is supported by thousands of exemplars found in the Dead Sea scroll fragments; the differences are not always errors of translation. The third family of manuscripts discovered apparently corresponds with the Samaritan Pentateuch, the holy book of the Samaritans. Two of the three strands of Biblical tradition were unknown to, ignored or rejected by Hebrew scholars who drew up the generally accepted Masoretic text around A.D. 100.

The finding of fragments of what must have been an amazing library of books, in a day when all books were written by hand, inevitably arouses keen interest in the question of who copied them. In the hope of finding some clue, excavations were commenced at a nearby ruin known as Khirbet Qumran, which had been assumed to be an old Roman fort occupied by soldiers of the Tenth Legion. The archeologist De Vaux undertook extensive exploration of this ruin in 1951 and continued his work in 1953–1956. It soon became evident that while Roman soldiers had lived among the ruins after the original buildings had burned, the communal buildings existed long before Roman times as the home of some two hundred people. The structure, about thirty by thirty-seven meters square, was of rough stone and was dominated by a large, two-storied tower. On the first floor was an auditorium and above it a room evidently used as a scriptorium or copying room. The remains of work tables were found there, two inkstands, one of copper and the other ceramic, and two plaster basins for washing. On the ground floor one large room was apparently utilized as a dining room and a smaller room near it as a kitchen. There were some seventeen hundred kitchen vessels carefully stacked according to size. The source of these vessels was uncovered nearby—the best preserved pottery factory yet found in Palestine, together with a pit for preparing clay and two ovens for firing. In addition, there were numerous pools apparently used for ritual purification. A large cemetery, containing the remains of over one thousand bodies, testified to extended occupancy of the community, and the discovery of over five hundred coins made it possible to fix accurately the periods in which people dwelt there.

A DEAD SEA SCROLL

The finding of these fragments of what must have been an amazing library inevitably aroused the questions of who had copied them. Research points most strongly to the sect of the Essenes.

Evidently the site was occupied during three periods. The silver coins dated from 110 to 37 B.C., from 4 B.C. until A.D. 68 and—after destruction of the building as indicated by a thick layer of black ash—from A.D. 68 to 100. Every indication urges the conclusion that the group who built and first occupied this building belonged to a Jewish sect called the Essenes. The last occupants were Roman troops.

In Josephus' Histories we find frequent references to the sect of the Essenes, whom he describes as being, together with the Pharisees and Sadducees, one of the three main Jewish sects. It is evident that he considers the Essenes the most to be admired. He claims that they "exceed all other men who addict themselves to virtue," holding all things in common, neither marrying wives nor keeping servants. While members of the sect live in every city, Josephus says, and are outstanding for their hospitality and virtue, there are also colonies of them where groups share a communal life. He speaks of their purifying baths, their simple food, their prayers before and after meat, their restraint in speech and conduct and their fondness for books and learning. He also describes the long probation imposed on candidates for the order and the oath of secrecy with which members are bound, their high standards of honesty and their piety toward God and justice toward man.

The substance of the Manual of Discipline closely parallels the principles of the Essenes as set forth by Josephus; the construction of the Qumran monastery fits exactly the needs of a sect living communally and devoted to the preservation of old books. The Essenes originated in the Maccabean era 175–132 B.C. and flourished until the fall of Jerusalem A.D. 70.

The recovery of the Essene books shedding light on their ideas and teachings has suggested to scholars that many of the teachings of the New Testament and some of its phraseology may have been drawn from Essene sources. Indeed some have gone so far as to hold that Jesus and his disciples were Essenes and that the Teacher of Righteousness referred to by the Essenes was a sort of pre-Christian Christ whose life, death and resurrection antedated Jesus of Nazareth and are the source of the teachings attributed to Jesus.

Certainly it is true that there are some striking similarities between the beliefs of the Essenes and those to be found in the Gospels. Let us list a few of them. Both Christians and Essenes regarded themselves as people of the new testament or covenant;

both considered love of God and love of neighbor as constituting the highest demands of spiritual law; both taught that there is a group of twelve who are elect of God and will be judges on the last day; both described members as being children of the light; both had a communal meal with prayer, and both a form of baptism; both felt they were living in the last days in which good and evil battle for supremacy and both stressed the importance of faith, truth and judgment. The Essene rule for dealing with an offender is strikingly similar to that given in the Book of Matthew. There is a similarity between the style of the Gospel of John and that of the book "The War of the Sons of Light and the Sons of Darkness." In the Gospel of John it is stated that the first disciples met Jesus on the lower Jordan not far from Khirbet Qumran, and it is entirely possible that his disciples had been in contact with the Essenes.

Nevertheless, while an association of the Essenes and Christians is not improbable, the differences between the two groups are even more numerous and significant than the similarities. Among these may be noted the following:

The Essenes believed the Mosaic covenant still binding; the Christians held it to be a shadow displaced by the substance.

The Essenes believed in salvation by strict obedience to the law, the Christians in salvation by faith.

The Essenes required an oath of allegiance; the Christian repudiated all oaths.

The Essenes expected Elijah or one like him to come and prepare the way for the Messiah; the Christians believed he had come in the person of John the Baptist.

The Essenes waited for two messiahs, the Messiah of Aaron and the Messiah of Israel; the Christians proclaimed that the true Messiah had come.

The Essenes had a carefully graded hierarchy, with the order of seating exactly stipulated; the Christians taught equality and superiority only in service.

The Essenes had a scrupulous regard for the ritual of the Sabbath that embraced the smallest detail; the Christians believed that faith in Christ superseded strict adherence to ritual.

The Essenes elaborately purified their bodies before taking meals; the Christians believed defilement was a matter of spiritual contamination and were criticized for taking meals without performing the usual purifying ablutions.

The Essenes practiced asceticism and did not encourage marriage; the Christians mixed freely in society and taught that marriage is of divine ordinance. The Essene "baptism" was a bath for the purpose of purification and obligatory twice a day. Christian baptism was a rite of initiation, signifying repentance and proclaiming one's act of faith.

The Christians, like the Essenes, had common meals, but the Lord's Supper was intended as a memorial to Christ's death and was not simply the taking of bread in company.

The Essenes taught hatred of enemies, and fought furiously against all who opposed them; the Christians taught love and forgiveness even toward enemies.

The Essenes were a group who kept apart, who accepted few recruits and then only after rigorous discipline. The Christian church was open to all and only asked a declaration of repentance and faith.

The Essenes ordinarily excluded women; the Christians welcomed them.

But of all the deductions that have been made about the relationship of the Essenes to Christianity, none seems more unwarranted than that which would make the Teacher of Righteousness a prototype of Christ. First of all, the Essene leader taught a new and stricter legalism than that of Moses himself. It was in no sense a Gospel. It was grim news of a much more intricate legal code than heretofore. Furthermore, there is not the slightest evidence for the assertion that the Teacher of Righteousness was crucified and rose again, but simply that the people "vexed" the Teacher of Righteousness. To deduce from this reference that he was crucified is an exercise of pure imagination. Nowhere is the Teacher referred to as the Messiah. He is not considered or called a Saviour, he is not believed to have risen from the dead, he is not expected to return at the end of the world. Indeed, it is not certain that any single person is to be identified as the Teacher. Some historians believe that a Teacher was appointed in every age, a recurring figure. It seems probable that instead of Jesus being a later echo of this unknown leader, the reverse may well be true: with the Bible before them, some scholars have read into the Teacher's life the events they find in the life of Jesus. Without the Bible as guide, they would not dream of such an interpretation. As Dr. Millar Burrows has pointed out, there is nothing in the reading of the Dead Sea scrolls that will undermine

Christian theology. No single teaching of Christianity has been in
any way affected by what has been found there. In the continuing
struggle of scholars to get back to the original text and meaning of
the Scriptures, the Qumran finds constitute the greatest stride in
one hundred years. Its full significance is yet to be known.


Another discovery hailed by some to rival in importance the
findings of the Dead Sea Scrolls was made in upper Egypt in 1945
or 1946. At that time peasants near a village called Khenaboskion
in the district of Nag Hamadi found a jar containing a number of
papyrus books in an old tomb cut from a limestone cliff. They were
found to constitute a complete Gnostic library, containing forty-
four treatises in the Coptic language bound in leather in thirteen
papyrus volumes. The manuscripts were apparently written in
the third or fourth century A.D. but are considered to be copies of
much older originals, some perhaps as early as the first half of the
second century. The most important for the Biblical scholar is a
document which is called the Gospel of Thomas. The title Gospel
is somewhat misleading; it is not a Gospel in the sense of being a
story of the life of Jesus. Rather it is a collection of alleged sayings
of Jesus, one hundred fourteen in all, without a narrative frame-
work. The sayings are introduced by the simple formula "Jesus
said," and have no special logical or chronological order. Before
discovery of the Book of Thomas, fourteen sayings quoted from
the Gospel of Thomas were known.

The Gospel of Thomas includes four types of sayings: many repeat word for word sayings contained in the four Gospels; others
provide variant readings of Gospel sayings; still others are not to
be found in the four Gospels but have been cited by church fathers;
and the last group, those which were unknown until now. The last
group of sayings are of the greatest interest; without doubt, there
will be endless discussion as to which, if any, can be considered
authentic. Some of the more striking are given below:

"Jesus said: If those who lead you say to you: Behold the kingdom is in Heaven, then the birds of heaven will precede you; if
they say to you that it is in the sea, then the fish will precede you.
But the Kingdom is within you and it is outside of you."

"His disciples said to him: Is circumcision useful or not? He said
to them if it had been useful, their father would have begotten

them circumcised from their mother on, but the true circumcision in spirit is alone advantageous."

"Mary said to Jesus: Whom are your disciples like? He said: They are like small children who have settled in a field which is not theirs. When the owners of the field come, they will say: Leave our field to us. They are completely naked in their presence so they will leave it to them and give them their field."

"Jesus said: Woe to them, the Pharisees, for they are like a dog lying in the manger of cattle, for he neither eats nor does he let the cattle eat."

"Jesus said: The kingdom of the Father is like a man who wanted to kill an important person; he drew his sword in the house, he pierced it through the wall to see if his hand would be steady, then he killed the important person."

The above information is taken from a lecture by Dr. Oscar Cullman, who has been studying the collection since 1956 and considers it to be of extreme importance in the interpretation of canonical Gospels. By the time the present book appears *The Gospel According to Thomas*, with translations from the original Coptic by G. Quispel and others, will have been published in the United States by Harper and Brothers.

# 16

# THE EARLY
# CHAPTERS
# OF LUKE

*Nazareth, Questions Regarding Luke
2:1-3, Bethlehem, Jerusalem*

IN REVIEWING THE FINDINGS OF ARCHEOLOGY AS THEY ILLUMINATE
the New Testament, we shall follow in general the order of the
Gospel of Luke, with occasional reference at the appropriate time
to places mentioned in the other Gospels. The Book of Luke opens
"in the days of Herod, king of Judea." To understand King Herod
and his background, let us turn back to 63 B.C. At this time two
brothers, Hyrcanus and Aristobolus II, were fighting each other for
the throne of Judea. Both men appealed to the Roman commander
Pompey for assistance. Pompey accepted the offer to mediate, entered the country and remained to rule. Judea was never again to
be free. When Julius Caesar defeated Pompey he made Antipater
the procurator, or governor, of Judea. Antipater's son Herod acted
as one of his deputies and soon displayed unusual executive abili-
ties. When Caesar was assassinated, war for the throne broke out
between Herod and Antigonus, the son of Aristobolus. Antigonus
appealed to the Parthians for help. They came and took Jerusalem.
This move alarmed the Romans, who drove out the Parthians and
in 40 B.C. made Herod the king of Judea.

Herod reigned for thirty-six years, or until 4 B.C. The first years
of his reign were difficult. It took three years of fighting to consoli-
date his kingdom. Mark Antony, the eastern ruler, presented Jeri-

cho and the coastal cities of Judea to Cleopatra, but when Antony
was defeated by Octavius the victor returned to Herod these cities
and additional territory.

Herod was one of the great builders of history. He rebuilt the
fallen city of Samaria, and named it Sebaste, the Greek for *Augustus,* in honor of the emperor. He greatly enlarged the city and
erected there a temple to Augustus. The temple had an impressive
approach, a massive stairway leading to a pillared platform. When
the ruins of the temple were excavated, archeologists found an altar at the foot of the stairway and beside it a fallen statue of Augustus. In city after city in the Near East, King Herod built temples
and broad avenues. The greatest of his self-assigned tasks was the
rebuilding of the holy temple in Jerusalem. Because he was an
Idumaean, a descendant of Esau, or Edom, brother of Jacob, and
because of his irreligious nature, there was considerable objection
to the project when he commenced, but Herod moved carefully in
order to avoid infringement upon the jealously guarded rights and
privileges of the Hebrew hierarchy. He himself refrained from entering the temple area and, so no unhallowed hand might defile
the work, sent a thousand priests to learn carpentry and masonry,
that they alone might enter the temple. Not to infringe on Hebrew
traditions, he caused the temple to be rebuilt on its original foundations, only making the walls much higher and more splendid. Work
on the main building was completed in eighteen months. The front
walls were ornamented with gold plate, as was the roof. The temple was described as "a snowy mountain covered with gold." Had
it stood it would be considered today one of the wonders of the
ancient world, but it was burned to the ground by Titus during the
conquest of Jerusalem A.D. 70.

King Herod was a brilliant, capable and brutal ruler. He was
able to maintain his throne under rival rulers and changed sides
as the interests of diplomacy dictated. He married a total of ten
wives, his favorite being Mariamne, granddaughter of Hyrcanus
II. When it was necessary for Herod to go to Rhodes to retain the
right to the throne and the issue of his journey was in doubt, he left
orders that his wife should be killed if he did not return. She
learned of this order and received him with marked coolness. Becoming suspicious of her reception of him, he had her executed in
a savage fit of jealousy, a deed he later was to view with great re-
morse. He also ordered the deaths of Mariamne's mother, brother

and grandmother, and later her two sons, on the suspicion that they were plotting against him. Before Herod died he gave orders that a large group of the leading Jews of the kingdom be gathered together and executed at the time of his death in order that Judea might mourn him, an order which was not carried out. His burial place, now in ruins, can be seen on Mount Frank where he erected a large fortress with circular towers and luxurious apartments.

The reign of Herod spans the transition from B.C. to A.D. Should Herod return and hear that an event in his reign marks the beginning of history for a large per cent of the human race, one wonders what event he would believe worthy of such note. Would he understand the significance of the birth of a baby to the wife of a village carpenter in Bethlehem? By his last will and testament Herod deeded Judea, Idumaea and Samaria to his son Archelaus, Galilee and Perea to Antipas and Transjordan to Philip. Augustus ratified the will with a single exception: he determined that Antipas and Philip should bear the title of tetrarch, not king as Herod had desired. Nevertheless, they were known as kings. The King Herod who later ordered the death of John the Baptist was Antipas, Herod's son. Thus Herod became a dynastic name.

### NAZARETH

Early in the Book of Luke is an account of the annunciation at Nazareth and of the return of Joseph and Mary to that place, the scene of the boyhood of Jesus the Nazarene. Placed high on a hill in Galilee, Nazareth is located in a cup-shaped hollow about a large spring now known as Mary's Well. From the hilltop behind the village one has a magnificent view of the countryside. To the west, Mount Carmel is clearly etched against the blue Mediterranean; to the northeast is stately Mount Hermon, snow-clad during much of the year, and to the east historic Mount Tabor where Barak assembled his forces under the direction of Deborah to fight against Sisera and defeated the Canaanites. In the time of Jesus, Nazareth lay on the main north-south road from the nearby metropolis, Sepphoris, and six miles north of the main east-west artery. The hillsides are steep but fertile; in spring they are covered with a glorious profusion of wild flowers. In a ten-minute stop when I passed through Nazareth several years ago I counted over thirty varieties of wild flowers. When Jesus was a boy Sepphoris was the largest

BYZANTINE MOSAICS

These mosaics were found in the Grottos of the Church of the
Annunciations at Nazareth. The first church on this site was
erected before A.D. 336.

city in all Galilee. It was a city set on a hill and embellished by Herod with notable buildings. During the boyhood of Jesus, Judas of Galilee seized Sepphoris in his rising against Rome. With a force of ten thousand Jews, Judas attacked Tiberias and secured arms. Then the Roman general Varus struck with his legions, the Jews were defeated, Sepphoris was burned to the ground, two thousand of its defenders were crucified around the smoking ruins and the remainder were taken as slaves to Rome. It was a time of flaming terror for the people of the region and left them with an indelible impression of Roman cruelty and might. For the boy Jesus a cross was a grim reality.

Archeologists from the University of Michigan have excavated Sepphoris and unearthed the ruins of a fort and a theater which were probably erected by Antipas when he later rebuilt the city.

### Questions Regarding Luke 2:1–3

It comes as a surprise to the reader to learn that each of the statements in the first three verses of Luke, Chapter 2, has been the center of considerable controversy among scholars. Long declared to be untrue was the statement in the first verse that Caesar Augustus ordered all the Roman world to be taxed; there was no written record of such enrollment in spite of the fact that the time of Caesar Augustus is dealt with in detail by several contemporary historians. The statement in the second verse, that Quirinius was then governor of Syria, was thought to have been disproved by a reference in the chronicles of Josephus which indicated that Quirinius had received the appointment about A.D. 6. The statement in the third verse, that each man was to return to his home city or village for taxation, was challenged as being incredible. It was argued that each man would have been enrolled where he was and not expected to travel many leagues to present himself at the proper poll. One writer went so far as to state that Luke put the whole world in commotion "in order to get Jesus born in Bethlehem." Archeology does much to settle the several questions of this controversy.

First of all archeological discoveries prove beyond doubt that regular enrollment of taxpayers was a feature of Roman rule and have shown that a census was taken every fourteen years. A large Egyptian papyrus, telling of an enrollment A.D. 174–175, refers to two previous enrollments, one in 160–161 and another in 146–147, at intervals of fourteen years. A much earlier papyrus, dated in the reign of Tiberius, reports a man's wife and dependents for enroll- ment and apparently has reference to a tax roll compiled A.D. 20–21. Another shows an enrollment under Nero A.D. 62–63; another lists those exempt from the poll tax in the forty-first year of Augustus, who began his reign in 27 B.C. Since Augustus records that he set about early in his reign to organize the empire, the first census may have been either in 23–22 B.C. or in 9–8 B.C.; the latter would be the census to which the Gospel of Luke refers. Obviously the first objection to Luke's account is no longer valid; there undoubtedly were regular enrollments when the Holy Land was a part of the Roman empire.

The exact history of the movements of Quirinius is still uncer- tain. At the city of Antioch in southern Galatia an inscription un- covered in 1912 was found to bear a number of names by which its date can be fixed as somewhere between 10 and 7 B.C. It bears the name of Quirinius, identifies him as prefect and records his election to the post of honorary duumvir, or magistrate, in recognition of his victory over the Hamonades, and proves that Quirinius was in the area as a commander at this date. He may, of course, have been twice in the district; or perhaps Josephus was in error in plac- ing the arrival at A.D. 6. Whatever the case, Quirinius was at Anti- och early enough to have been governor at the time of a census when Jesus was born. The Gospel of Luke in calling this the first census, implies at least a second census at a later time.

A papyrus found in Egypt giving directions for the conduct of a census affords an adequate reply to the question of whether a man had to return to his native town to be counted. It reads: "Because of the approaching census it is necessary that all those residing for any cause away from their homes should at once prepare to return to their own governments in order that they may complete the fam- ily registration of the enrollment and that tilled lands may retain those belonging to them." Thus there is convincing evidence that the Gospel of Luke is correct in this regard. For each one of the ob- jections historians have made, archeology has provided a reason- able reply.

## BETHLEHEM

At Bethlehem, some six miles south of the city of Jerusalem, the chief interest of the Christian today centers upon the Church of the Nativity built on the presumed site of the Saviour's birth. Have we any way of identifying this as the authentic location? It is known that the original church on the site was constructed on the order of Constantine. Queen Helena, mother of Constantine, visited the Holy Land when she was eighty and dedicated the church built over the mystic grotto where Christ is said to have been born.

Later generations saw the enlargement and beautification of this church. It is said to be the oldest church in continuous use in the world. The tradition that this is the place of the nativity is very old. Justin Martyr, a native of Palestine, wrote between 155–160: "... when the child was born in Bethlehem, since Joseph could not find a lodging in that village he took up his quarters in a certain cave near the village."* Origen, in 246–248, wrote: "there is shown at Bethlehem the cave where he was born and the manger in the cave where he was wrapped in swaddling clothes. And this sight is greatly talked of in surrounding places, even among the enemies of the faith, it being said that in this cave was born that Jesus who is worshipped and reverenced by the Christians."† Jerome says that from the time of Hadrian, 117–138, the birth spot was overshadowed by a grove dedicated to Adonis and in the very cave where the infant Christ uttered his earliest cry, lamentation was made for the paramour of Venus. Because Hadrian made a point of desecrating Christian shrines, tradition would indicate that as early as his reign this particular spot was hallowed as the place of the miraculous birth.

The church built by Constantine was pulled down at the order of the Emperor Justinian and a larger church constructed A.D. 527–565. Justinian gave orders that a building be erected so magnificent that not even the temple at Jerusalem would rival it. When he came to inspect the completed church, he was bitterly disappointed and ordered the man in charge to be punished. The building stills stands; its nave is thought to be a part of the original structure. It was spared by the Persians who conquered Palestine in 614, we are told, because of a mosaic at the entrance showing the coming of the Wise Men (dressed in Persian costume). The Moslems also spared it although the Fatimid Khalif Al Hakim destroyed most of the Christian churches in Palestine in 1009. On Christmas Day, 1101, the crusader Baldwin I of Flanders succeeded his

* Quoted in Finegan, *op. cit.*, p. 439.
† *Ibid.*

brother and was crowned in this church as king of Jerusalem. In the twelfth century other crusaders enriched it with splendid mosaic decorations. In 1934 the archeologist Harvey was given permission to carry out limited excavations and under the floor of the present church discovered remains of Constantine's church. Harvey was able to reconstruct its original plan and uncovered a strip of flooring paved with patterned mosaics, the oldest mosaics yet found in Palestine. In the ancient church of Santa Pudenziana in Rome is a mosaic, probably dating from late in the fourth century, which pictures what archeologists believe to be the Church of the Nativity. If so, this gives us a contemporary view of the original church of Constantine.

## JERUSALEM

Jesus made his first visit to Jerusalem as a boy of twelve, according to the account in the Gospel of Luke. Old Jerusalem is so deeply buried in the rubble of centuries, in most places to a depth of forty to seventy feet, that very little of the old city remains, and it is difficult to visualize how it must have presented itself to Jesus as a boy. In Jesus' time the city was almost divided by the Tyropoeon Valley, which is now only a minor depression. Approaching from the north, Jesus would have passed through two concentric walls that guarded the city on that side. Herod Agrippa added a third wall but it was not completed before A.D. 70. It seems probable that the Church of the Holy Sepulcher was outside the second wall and inside the third, and later, wall.* But so complete has been the destruction of the city that this supposition is a matter of dispute. If it was inside, the crucifixion must have occurred elsewhere and Golgotha was not on the spot covered by the church.

Herod the Great built, or rebuilt, the wall, strengthening it with three magnificent towers, one seventy-three feet high, one one hundred and seventeen and one one hundred thirty-one feet. Josephus claims that these towers were of a strength and magnitude and beauty without parallel anywhere in the world. Herod also beautified his capital city by the erection of a theater, a hippodrome and an amphitheater. In imitation of Grecian custom Herod proclaimed

* The description which follows of the Church of the Holy Sepulcher is based on an account given by George E. Wright, *Biblical Archaeology* (Philadelphia: Westminster Press, 1957), p. 224.

St. Stephen's Gate

This gate, in the fortress-like wall surrounding the Old City of Jerusalem, was named for Stephen, who was stoned to death nearby. The wall is about twenty feet high and is two and a half miles long.

that there would be a contest of games at Jerusalem every five years. Notices of the athletic contest were sent to neighboring countries and peoples, and rich prizes were offered to the winners. All about the amphitheater were inscriptions in gold and silver in honor of Caesar. Wild beasts were gathered from distant mountains, and men under condemnation of death were sent into the arena to fight them. Thus the city which Jesus saw as a boy was a magnificent one, splendid, barbarous and cruel.

The temple to God, or Yahweh, was the most impressive of the buildings in Jerusalem. Historians believe it was on the site of the present Harim es Sharif, where stands the beautiful Dome of the Rock, sometimes mistakenly called the mosque of Omar. Herod the Great had enclosed the temple hill on three sides with great walls made of huge stones carefully fitted together. Known as the wailing wall, where Jewish patriots before the late war with the Arabs mourned the lost glory of the temple, it is a notable example of Herodian masonry. The temple was composed of an inner and an outer court. The walls of the inner court were lined with porticoes, cloisters and double lines of marble columns roofed over by a ceiling of cedar richly carved. Josephus says that these were the work of King Solomon; this is likely Solomon's porch, mentioned in John 10:23, the place where the disciples gathered after the healing of the lame man (Acts 3:11). To the south were the royal porticoes supported by one hundred sixty-two columns, each so large that three men, touching hands, could barely reach around one of them. The inner court was separated from the outer by an elaborately carved stone balustrade of exquisite workmanship. At regular intervals the balustrade bore signs warning foreigners not to cross to the inner court on pain of death: "No foreigner may enter within the balustrade or enclosure around the sanctuary. Whoever is caught will render himself liable to the death penalty which will inevitably follow." It was the outer court which Jesus cleansed by driving out the money-changers from the house of prayer for all nations (Mark 11:17).

The temple was approached by nine magnificent gates. One of these was ornamented with beautifully wrought brass. The double door was some forty-five by twenty-two and one-half feet. Another, the "Beautiful Gate" as it was called, was some seventy-five feet high and adorned with thick plates of gold and silver, as were other gates. The entire structure was a work of dazzling magnificence.

# 17

# THE SCENES OF THE MINISTRY OF JESUS

*The River Jordan, The Sea of Galilee, Tyre, Transjordan and Jerusalem, Bethany, Calvary and the Holy Sepulcher*

## THE RIVER JORDAN

THERE IS NO OTHER RIVER ON EARTH THAT FLOWS AT SO LOW A LEVEL. There are four main sources of the Jordan, three flowing from the base of Mount Hermon and the fourth pouring in its waters from the west. They flow through a shallow lake called the Waters of Merom and plunge rapidly to the Sea of Galilee. Between these two bodies the Jordan crosses sea level and by the time it reaches the Sea of Galilee it is some six hundred and ninety-six feet below sea level. Leaving the Sea of Galilee it follows an amazingly tortuous course down to the Dead Sea, flowing two hundred miles in order to compass a distance of sixty-five miles. The total drop between the seas is five hundred and ninety feet, at a rate of about nine feet to every direct mile. Inevitably the waters run swiftly, and the course of the river, flowing between high mud banks, is constantly changing. There are many whirlpools, rapids and small cascades. The river is ninety to one hundred feet wide and from three to ten feet deep. Near the Sea of Galilee the water is fresh and clear, but as the Jordan goes on it gathers an increasing load of silt in its lower reaches. One can well understand how Naaman the Syrian, accustomed to the crystalline rivers of Abana and Pharpar at Damascus, would look at the Jordan with scorn and say "Are not the waters of Abana and Pharpar better than all the rivers of Israel? Cannot I wash in them and be clean?"

Between Galilee and the Dead Sea the Jordan flows through a country of lush vegetation. Dense, almost impenetrable thickets of willows, oleanders, reeds, poplars and tamarisks grow in great profusion. Before the advent of the archeologists, many travelers to the Holy Land expressed the opinion that the valley could never have been thickly populated; the combination of heat and malaria, savage men and wild animals would have made it a forbidding place. On the other hand, the Bible story of Abraham and Lot indicates that the valley of the Jordan was at one time well populated. The archeologist's spade has again sustained the Bible picture, showing that large and small settlements dotted the land. Excellent early pottery reveals an advanced civilization. There was intensive agriculture, with an elaborate system of dams, irrigation ditches and underground aqueducts. On the east side of the Jordan alone, over seventy settlements have been discovered and explored, many of them founded as much as five thousand years ago, at a time when the valley was one of the richest regions in Palestine. Whereas today Transjordan has about 350,000 inhabitants, Nelson Glueck estimates that in the time of Christ there were probably a million and a half living there. Thus the Jordan Valley was a populous place, excellent as a center for the preaching of John the Baptist. There are no less than eleven perennial streams flowing through the area to Jordan and the Dead Sea. Glueck comments on the long traditions of the tribes living there today; there are old men who can repeat their tribal traditions which have descended through forty generations, over a thousand years. If they should stray in recounting these long-held traditions, they are at once corrected by those listening. Oral tradition may still be detailed and accurate, even when committed to the page long after its inception—or never written at all.

## THE SEA OF GALILEE

The Sea of Galilee is a lovely pear-shaped body of water about thirteen miles long and eight miles wide at its widest point. Its depth varies from the shallow beach waters to a depth of over a hundred and fifty feet. On a clear day it is a deep blue mirror in a green bowl. When cloud banks to the east turn red at sunset, Galilee looks like a "sea of glass mingled with fire," as described in Revelation 15:2. Because of the sharp difference in altitude—Mount Hermon is nearly ten thousand feet above sea level and the Sea of Galilee is seven hundred feet below—the sea is liable to sudden and violent storms caused by powerful winds sweeping down the steep valleys. The surrounding hills are fertile and watered by many springs. In the time of Jesus there were nine towns of considerable size around the lake, including some of the fairest in the Near East. They contained temples, synagogues, palaces, hippodromes and bathhouses, for the most part of marble and in the Grecian style. There was an abundance of fruits and vegetables in the region. The sea provided constant catches of fish which were packed in brine and shipped even as far as Rome.

Of these many cities, the first mentioned in the Gospels is Tiberias, referred to in John 6:23. It was built by Herod the Great and was the main fortress in Galilee. In order to complete the city, Herod ordered the removal of an ancient cemetery. For this reason the city was considered unclean by pious Jews, who scrupulously avoided it. If compelled to enter Tiberias by some urgent necessity, they believed that they became ritually unclean and would have to undergo seven days of purification. The city at that time was avoided by the devout. After the fall of Jerusalem, it became the chief center of Jewish learning and the location of the Jewish Sanhedrin. The Palestinian Talmud was completed there. Herod the Great built splendid palaces on the adjacent hills. There black ruins and shattered masonry can still be seen. Tiberias was famous also for its hot springs, considered to have medicinal benefit. Shortly before his death Herod visited the springs in the hope of finding a cure. The waters still flow and attract invalids to Tiberias. There is no record that Jesus ever visited the place.

To the north and west of Tiberias are two mountain peaks, about two thousand feet high, known as the Horns of Hattin. They are the cones of extinct volcanoes and are thought to be the site of the Sermon on the Mount. The location offers a commanding view of the lake below. It is equally renowned as the battlefield where the Crusaders were defeated in 1187. Cut off from the lake by Saladin, they fought with desperate fury until all but a few had perished. Those taken prisoner were executed. As George Adam Smith expressed it, here "a militant and truculent Christianity, as false as

TIBERIAS

On the western shore of the Sea of Galilee, this picturesque old city was built about A.D. 21 by Herod Antipas. It is one of the four sacred cities of the Jews, the others being Jerusalem, Hebron and Safad.

the relics of the 'True Cross' round which it was rallied, met its judicial end within view of the scenes where Christ proclaimed the Gospel of Peace and went about doing good."* Here also the warning "They that take the sword shall perish with the sword," received grim fulfillment.

Three miles north of Tiberias on the lake was the city of Magdala, the home of Mary Magdalene. Lying at the southern edge of the plain of Genessaret, it is known today as Magdal. In the time of Jesus it was a city of forty thousand and famous as a center of the dyeing industry.

From ancient times the plains of Genessaret have been lauded for their fertility. Josephus praised it in the highest terms.

Its nature is wonderful as well as its beauty. Its soil is so fertile that all sorts of trees can grow upon it; for the temper of the air is so well mixed that it agrees very well with those several sorts. Particularly walnuts, which require the coldest air, flourish there in vast plenty; there are palm trees also, which grow best in a hot climate; fig trees and olives grow near them which require an air that is temperate. One may call this place the ambition of nature which forces those plants that are naturally enemies to one another to agree together; it is a happy contention of the seasons, as if each one of them laid claim to this country, for it not only nourishes different sorts of autumnal fruits beyond man's expectations, but preserves them a great while; it supplies men with the principal fruits, with grapes and figs continually during ten months of the year.

In such an idyllic surrounding how natural and impressive must have been the parables of the sowers, the reapers, the growing wheat, the lilies of the field, and the mild rain that—perhaps as Jesus spoke—fell on the just and the unjust!

On the northwest corner of the lake lay Capernaum. For most of Jesus' Galilean ministry Capernaum was his chief center of work. It was here that Jesus taught in the synagogue on the Sabbath and healed the lunatic, here he cured the fever that plagued Peter's mother-in-law, here the sick crowded to his door and he healed them. It was here that the paralytic carried by four was lowered through the roof to be healed, and here Jesus cured the centurion's

* George Adam Smith, *Historical Geography of the Holy Land* (London: Hodder and Stoughton, 1920), p. 441.

SYNAGOGUE

Called Christ's "own city" (Matthew 9:1), Capernaum was the
many miracles of healing. The synagogue shown was fifty by

AT CAPERNAUM

center of Jesus' Galilean ministry. Here he taught and performed
seventy feet surrounded on three sides by a pillared colonnade.

slave. It was against the city of Capernaum that Jesus pronounced his warning woe (Luke 10:15). The site of this historic city has been identified as being under the ruins of Tell Hum, the most extensive ruins on the west side of the lake. The most significant discovery was of a ruined synagogue, excavated by German archeologists and partly restored by Franciscan monks. The imposing limestone structure faced Jerusalem, in deference to the instructions of the rabbis that all synagogues face that city, a custom that archeologists have shown to be generally observed. Inasmuch as both Titus, the Roman general, A.D. 70, and Hadrian, the Roman emperor, A.D. 130, ordered the destruction of synagogues, it seems probable that this synagogue was built at a later time, perhaps as late as A.D. 200, although some scholars consider it a first-century building. In whatever event, precedent and piety would call for it to be rebuilt on the exact site of an earlier temple. One side of the building, overlooking the lake, had three doors and a large window from which, one imagines, restless boys watched the fishing boats on the water when they tired of the ritual.

The interior of the synagogue was fifty by seventy feet and surrounded on three sides by a pillared colonnade. A separate, upper section was designated as a gallery for women. Certain parts of the building are shown by inscriptions to have been donated by individuals. One fragment of a pillar still bears the inscription "Zebedee, the son of John." In the Bible mention is made of John the son of Zebedee. Because it was a common custom to alternate a pair of names from generation to generation, it is well within the range of possibility that the pillar was donated by some later member of the family of John the Apostle. The Roman eagle is included in the figures used for ornamentation—strange to see if one recalls the hatred felt by the Hebrews for the Romans. May it not be that the eagle was placed there by the Roman centurion who loved the Jews and built for them the Capernaum synagogue, as told in the Gospel of Luke, Chapter 7:2–5?

At a place called Ain Tabgha, southwest of Capernaum, is to be seen the ruins of a fourth-century church known as the Church of the Loaves and the Fishes. No one knows when the original church was erected; probably it was built in Roman times and later rebuilt. All that is left today is a pavement and the stumps of a few broken pillars. H. V. Morton, in his book *In the Steps of the Master*, describes his visit to this church in these words:

The old Bedouin who guards the precious relic took up a broom and swept away the covering of earth, and with each sweep exquisite little pictures flashed into the sunlight. The floor was formed of small delicately tinted mosaics in which blue and green predominated. The artist, whoever he was, knew and loved the bird life of the Sea of Galilee and rendered it in his little colored stones in a most affectionate way. The pavement is divided into a number of squares, about the size of an average carpet, and each square is a design of decorative birds and animals, but so lovingly done, and with a sly sense of humor too, that one can imagine the creator of this pavement hiding in the lakeside reeds smiling to himself as he watched the often absurd movements of the ducks and cranes and the self assured twittering little birds that hung in the rushes. I like his picture of an extraordinarily smug goose pulling a lotus flower. Then there was another spirited picture, a fight between a heron and a serpent. There were also plump quail. And I admired the astonishing skill he showed in capturing, in what one would imagine to be an intractable material, that sudden moment when a water fowl stands up in the water and flaps its wings just once or twice, like a man yawning and stretching his arms. It is just a flash and it is gone.*

In Luke 10:13–15 Christ pronounced woes against the cities of Chorazin and Bethsaida, and against Capernaum, in a way that suggests these places were close together. Less than two miles north of the ruins of Capernaum is Kerazeh which is probably the site of Chorazin. Here too the chief ruin is that of a synagogue. It is richly ornamented with sculptures of animals and representations of grape-gathering and pressing. The city of Bethsaida lay to the east of the Jordan. Rebuilt by Philip and renamed Julias after the daughter of the emperor, it was renowned as a large and important city. Where it lay we cannot tell; there is only an uncertain identification with a rocky hillside. How literally and terribly has Christ's prediction of its destruction been fulfilled!

To the north and on the Mediterranean is the site of the ancient city of Tyre, a city that appears again and again in Biblical records and ancient inscriptions. The name *Tyre* means rock, and the name is both typical of the site of the city—for it was, like Rome, founded on a rock—and of its strength and stability. The rock on which it

* H. V. Morton, *In the Steps of the Master* (New York: Dodd, Mead, 1934), p. 242.

Religious News Service Photo

BEACH AT TYRE

Tyre on the Mediterranean appears again and again in Biblical records
and ancient inscriptions. Tyre means *rock* and is typical of both the site
of the city and of its stability and strength. It was once the greatest
center of trade in the Near East.

was built was an island about half a mile from shore. The original name of the city was Ushu, and we find the city mentioned in the Tell el-Amarna letters. It was founded as a colony by the city of Sidon, and it became in time the greatest center of trade in the Near East. In late years King Hiram, who had so much to do with King Solomon's building operations, ordered the construction of a causeway between the city and the mainland. At that time Tyre was supreme in arts and crafts among all the cities of the ancient kingdoms. So it was that King Solomon sent messengers to King Hiram, reminding him that "thou knowest that there is not among us any that can skill to hew timber like unto the Sidonians" (I Kings 5:6), and saying that Solomon depended upon King Hiram and his craftsmen for the intricate and massive bronze work of the temple. The ill-famed Jezebel, who tried so viciously to stamp out the worship of Yahweh, was a native of Tyre, the daughter of King Ethbaal. As queen to King Ahab, she inspired his evil plans. In the Book of Ezekiel, Chapter 27, is a vivid description of the varied riches of Tyre and of its commerce with all nations: silver, iron, tin and lead, horns of ivory and ebony, emeralds, purple and embroidered work, fine linen, coral and agate, spices, precious stones and gold; and the prediction of its total destruction. But so strong was its island position that for centuries Tyre seemed impregnable. The great Assyrian monarch, Shalmaneser V, besieged the city for five years, yet failed to capture the island city, although he did capture the old city on the mainland. The great Babylonian king, Nebuchadnezzar, invested the city for no less than thirteen years and was forced to withdraw. With a powerful navy and ready access to supplies from the sea, Tyre seemed invulnerable; but Alexander the Great was to succeed where others had failed. When his demand that the city be surrendered was refused because of the Tyrians' loyalty to their ruler, the King of Persia, Alexander launched a furious attack on the city. Realizing that he would be unable to overcome the city from the sea, he ordered the old portion of the city on the mainland torn down and with the rubble commenced a great causeway some two hundred feet wide, reaching out into the sea toward the island. On this causeway he erected war engines and high towers. The Tyrians attacked from the sea, employing a mixture of burning naphtha and sulphur, hurled red-hot sand from their catapults and set fire to the towers and destroyed them. Aware of the need for adequate sea power, Alexander gathered together all available shipping. A sea battle ensued in which Alexander again met defeat. However, land victories over the Persians and growing fear of his might, turned the tide. The king of Cyprus threw in his lot with Alexander and sent to his support a great fleet of two hundred ships. The attack was launched from floating batteries; at the end of seven months the walls were scaled, some ten thousand Tyrians were slaughtered and thirty thousand were sold into slavery.

The city of Tyre was gradually restored. Herod the Great built a temple there and the Apostle Paul spent a week on a ship in the harbor while the crew discharged cargo. In the second century it became the see of a bishop. The first Christian church to be built there was destroyed in later persecutions. At the time Constantine the Great was converted, a great basilica was built at Tyre. At the dedication of the basilica A.D. 316 the church historian Eusebius delivered an oration. An outer colonnaded court surrounded a fountain. The church had great triple doors leading to the church proper, which was paved with marble and roofed with carved cedar. A document entitled the "Apostolic Constitutions" gives a vivid account of the Christian church and its form of worship as practiced in the days of Tyre:

Let the building be long with its head to the east, with its vestries on both sides of the east end, and so it will be like a ship. In the middle let the bishop's throne be placed, and on each side of him let the presbytery sit down; and let the deacon stand near at hand, with closely girt garments, for they are like the mariners and managers of the ship. In accordance with their arrangement, let the laity sit on the other side with all quietness and good order. And let the women sit by themselves, they also keeping silence. In the middle let the reader stand upon some high place; let him read the books of Moses . . . and the Epistles of Paul . . . and the Gospels. . . . In the next place, let the presbyters one by one, not all together, exhort the people, and the bishop in the last place, as being the commander. Let the porters stand at the entrances of the men and give heed to them, while the deaconesses stand at those of the women, like shipmen. . . . But if anyone be found sitting out of his place, let him be rebuked by the deacon, as a manager of the foreship, and removed into the place proper for him; for the church is not only like a ship, but also like a sheepfold. For as the shepherds place all the brute creatures distinctly . . . so is it to be in the church. Let the young men sit by themselves if there be a place for them, but if not let them stand upright. Let those already advanced in years sit in order and let the children stand beside their mothers and fathers. Let the younger women also sit by themselves if there be a place for them but if not let them stand behind the elder women. Let those women who are married and have children be placed by themselves, while the virgins and the widows and the elderwomen stand or sit before all the rest. Let the deacon be the disposer of the places, that every one of those that comes in may go to his proper place and not sit at the entrance. In like manner let the deacon oversee the people that nobody may whisper nor slumber nor laugh nor nod, for all ought in the church to stand wisely and soberly and attentively, having their attention fixed upon the word of the Lord. After this, let all rise up with one consent and looking towards the east, after the catechumens and penitents are gone out, pray to God eastward. . . . As to the deacons, after the prayer is over, let some of them attend upon the oblation of the eucharist, ministering to the Lord's body with fear. Let others of them watch the multitude and keep them silent. But let that deacon who is at the high priest's hand say to the people, "Let no one have a quarrel against another; let no one come in hypocrisy." Then let the men give the men, and the women give the women, the Lord's kiss. . . . After this let the deacon pray for the whole church, for the whole world. . . . Let the bishop pray for the people. After this let the sacrifice follow, the people standing and praying silently; and when the oblation has been made, let every rank by itself partake of the Lord's body and precious blood in order, and approach with reverence and holy fear, as to the body of their king. Let the women approach with their heads covered, as is becoming the order of women; but let the door be watched, lest any unbeliever, or one not yet initiated, come in.*

The city of Tyre continued to flourish into the time of the Crusaders, who used it as a base for their military operations. But after the fall of Acre and the reconquest of Palestine by the Saracens, Tyre was totally destroyed and has remained a ruin till this day. Many were the predictions of its fall; not only Ezekiel, but Isaiah Jeremiah, Amos and Zechariah had added their predictions to his. Zechariah's prophecy in Chapter 9:4 is typical: "Behold, the Lord will cast her out, and he will smite her power in the sea; and she shall be devoured with fire." So complete was the overthrow of

* Quoted in Finegan, *op. cit.*, pp. 416-417.

Tyre that in our own day Kipling uses the fate of the city as a warning in "Recessional":

> Far-called, our navies melt away;
> On dune and headland sinks the fire:
> Lo, all our pomp of yesterday
> Is one with Nineveh and Tyre!

## TRANSJORDAN AND JERUSALEM

One of the most beautiful sections of Palestine in the time of
Jesus was the so-called Decapolis, or ten cities. They were Greek
cities, all but one lying east of the Jordan. Typical of these cities is
Gerasa, characterized by one archeologist as "the most satisfactory
ruins I have ever seen." Gerasa was fifty miles southeast of the Sea
of Galilee, on a branch of the river Jabbok. It was one of the most
brilliant cities of Transjordan, possessed of fine colonnaded streets,
a circular forum and beautiful temples, theaters and public baths.
It is not to be confused with the country of the Gerasenes, mentioned in Luke 8:26, where the demon-possessed were healed; that
place is probably to be identified with Kersa, on the east side of
Galilee, near steep hills plunging into the sea.

In Gerasa, the remains of an immense circus for gladiatorial combats can be seen. There was an extraordinary artificial lake, three
hundred by seven hundred feet, where, high in the hills, mock naval
battles were fought. The main street of Gerasa was over half a mile
long, its pavement deeply rutted by chariot wheels. The sidewalks
were raised above the street. There was a complete underground
drainage system and an exquisite Greek theater, the latter so well
preserved that even the numbering of the tiers of seats is still legible. Half-way down are two tiers of elaborately carved seats, obviously box seats for distinguished personages. The stage is over
one hundred feet wide, giving ample space for impressive spectacles. The ruins of the temple of Artemis has a portico with huge
pillars carved of a rosy limestone forty-five feet high and five feet
thick.

On the steep winding road running from Jericho to Jerusalem
one can see the so-called Inn of the Good Samaritan. It is the only
inn along this road, and its stones show that it was built in Roman
times or even earlier. Some fragmentary mosaics appear to be the

remnants of a Christian chapel. Like other caravansary in the Near East, it consists of an oblong-shaped series of walls and buildings surrounding an open courtyard. In the middle of the court is a well. Whether the story of the Good Samaritan is simply a parable, or whether it is an account of an actual incident, is uncertain. This may well have been the inn Jesus mentioned.

## BETHANY

The settlement of Bethany was undoubtedly on the eastern slope of the Mount of Olives where the present village called el-Azari-yeh, the place of Lazarus, is located. In the center of the present town stands a mosque built over the ruins of a Christian church, which in turn stood over a cave pointed out as the tomb of Lazarus. After the Moslems took Palestine, Christians were refused access to the cave and the entrance was blocked with masonry. In the seventeenth century, a Father Custos secured permission for Christians to enter once again. Today one finds twenty steps leading down a dark dusty cave where, two steps lower still, is a small tomb claimed to be that of Lazarus. In Bethany today, as H. V. Morton put it, "houses look like ruins and ruins look like houses." Here are shown the supposed dwelling places of Mary and of Simon, but these cannot be authentic. It was here on the hillside, near enough to be accessible to Jerusalem in a village with a beautiful view over the Jordan and the hills of Moab, that Jesus found the only home he knew after leaving his own. Here the practical Martha cared for his physical needs and the mystical Mary refreshed his spirit by her eagerness to learn. Their brother Lazarus was recalled to Jesus as "he whom you love," and the Gospel of John tells us it was the raising of Lazarus from the dead that brought the wrath of the rulers upon Jesus.

The last days of the ministry of Jesus centered largely about Herod's glorious temple. In Luke 21:5 reference is made to the "goodly stones" with which it had been built. The largest of these so far found is sixteen and one-half feet long and thirteen feet across; Josephus tells us that still greater stones, thirty-seven and one-half by twelve by eighteen, were also a part of the temple structure. Of this magnificent building the rabbis were wont to declare: "He who hath not seen Jerusalem in its beauty, has not seen a beautiful city,

Inn of the Good Samaritan. These ruins of an ancient

inn are found on the road from Jericho to Jerusalem.

and who has not seen the building of the second temple has not seen a handsome building in his life." Before it stood the great altar of sacrifice.

The enormous amount of masonry that went into the temple and its attendant structures can be estimated from the fact that from the outside base of the wall in the valley to the top of the temple was nearly five hundred feet. The source of this enormous quantity of rock is referred to by Josephus as being the royal quarry, but the location of the quarry was lost sight of for many centuries. Just over a century ago, an Englishman named Barclay, with dog and gun, was walking outside the walls of Jerusalem near the Damascus gate when his dog suddenly vanished into a hole. After some delay the dog crawled into view. Barclay found the entrance to a cave under the city wall. The next day he returned with a party of men, widened the opening, and came upon a weird and terrifying scene. They found themselves in a vast cavern, so great that the light of their torches could not penetrate its furthest recesses. Barclay realized that they had rediscovered the royal quarry which, from the time of King Solomon, had been the source of building material for Jerusalem, a vast opening with cliffs, wells and high passages leading back into the mountain. It is estimated that enough stone has been removed from the heart of the mountain to build three times over all of modern Jerusalem. The stone is a peculiar white which when first cut is soft, but which rapidly hardens when exposed to air. Today one can see the marks of the tools of the ancient Phoenician stonecutters made twenty-eight hundred years ago and looking as clear and fresh as if carved yesterday. Visitors often fancy that the masons will be back at any moment. It is thought than an underground passageway leads from the quarry to the temple and that the ark, together with other riches of the temple, was hidden in the quarry when the temple was destroyed by Nebucadnezzar in 587 B.C. From the carvings on the Arch of Titus in Rome, we know that at least some of the riches remained to be carried off as plunder at the time of the final destruction of the temple A.D. 70.

## CALVARY AND THE HOLY SEPULCHER

The sites of the death and resurrection of Jesus have long been identified with the area covered by the Church of the Holy Sepul-

TOMB OF LAZARUS

A native boy stands reverently before the traditional tomb of Lazarus,
in Bethany on the slope of the Mount of Olives a few
miles from Jerusalem.

cher. It will be remembered that the city of Jerusalem was completely destroyed by Titus the Roman A.D. 70. Josephus says that in this disaster 1,100,000 Jews were killed and 97,000 sold into slavery. The Christians, in obedience to the warning of Christ, fled the city and escaped to Pella in Transjordan and survived. Titus made of Jerusalem a desolation. Apart from the western walls, left standing to testify to the heroism of the soldiers who had conquered such a city, all other walls were leveled so completely that no trace remains. A visitor reported that "there was nothing to make those who came hither believe it had ever been inhabited." Later, the city was slowly rebuilt. Many Christians came back in the course of time, rebuilding so far as was possible on the old sites, and perhaps identifying Golgotha and the tomb.

In the year 122 the Emperor Hadrian visited Jerusalem and decreed that the city should be rebuilt. It was to be a purely Roman city, Aelia Capitalina. Anticipating the desecration of the temple site, the Jews rose in protest. So bitterly did they fight that Hadrian was compelled to send for Julius Severus, his ablest general. By the conquest of six hundred fortified towns and villages and the slaughter of 580,000 men, the rising was put down and the rebuilding of Jerusalem proceeded. Hadrian ordered that a pagan temple be erected on the site of Golgotha. He surrounded the hill of Golgotha with a twenty-foot wall, filled in the spaces with rubble and concrete, and made a platform for the temple three hundred feet long and one hundred sixty feet wide. The platform was planted with trees; a statue of Jupiter was erected over the sepulcher and a statue of Venus over Calvary. It remained so for two hundred years, until Rome was conquered and the emperor surrendered to the Christian church. Orders came from Rome to Macarius, bishop of Jerusalem, to restore the church on Calvary. In the year 336, the heathen temple was pulled down and a tomb beneath it disclosed. Apparently the ecclesiastical historian Eusebius, a boy at the time, was present when this occurred. Another writer connects the restoration with the visit of the emperor's mother, Helena, at a later date. Certainly Helena visited Jerusalem and thought she had discovered the True Cross in a nearby cistern. She had the masonry surrounding Golgotha cleared away and erected a splendid rotunda above it. The supposed hill of Golgotha, as it remained, was a small mound of about eighteen by fifteen feet. In later days the church was burned, rebuilt and again destroyed. In the days of the Crusaders it was rebuilt on a grand scale. At various times it has been remodeled and repaired; parts of the present church date from the Crusades.

One may spend days exploring the confusing labyrinth of chapels and shrines in the present church. Much is old and dirty, much is trivial and tawdry. Due to the bitter rivalry between various Christian sects, every inch of the church is staked off by custom and tradition, the smallest picture and piece of carpet claimed by some special group, and any transgression on the rights of others is likely to result in rioting.

Six churches—the Orthodox, the Armenian Gregorian, the Coptic, the Syrian, the Abyssinian and the Roman—at present have a share in the church. For a time during the Crusades the Roman church was in complete control. Little by little the other groups bought their way in. The supposed sepulcher itself is covered by an ornate shrine in the center of the church in which just forty-three lamps are allowed to be hung, thirteen by the Roman, thirteen by the Orthodox, thirteen by the Armenians and four by the Abyssinians.

Typical of the superstition surrounding this ancient shrine is the annual ceremony of the holy fire. It is based on a tradition that centuries ago the monk whose duty it was to keep the lamp burning in the shrine of the holy sepulcher fell asleep and allowed the lamp to go out. He was overwhelmed with grief and horror at his sin and pleaded so earnestly for forgiveness that fire was sent down from heaven and the lamp was relighted on high. Thereafter, each year during the Easter season, the miracle is re-enacted. The great church is thronged by thousands of believers, each holding an unlighted candle in his hand. With great pomp and ceremony the archbishop of the Orthodox church thrice circumambulates the sepulcher. In lavishly rich robes, bearing gaudy banners and singing stately anthems, the group of priests makes its way through the crowded assembly. Then the archbishop enters the sepulcher alone, carrying in his hand a large bundle of unlighted candles. There is a sudden flash and the archbishop emerges from the shrine with candles lit. Eagerly the crowd strains forward, each striving to light his candle from the holy flame. They scatter through the narrow streets of the city, each carefully protecting his burning candle until he reaches home. Lighting one candle from another, the holy fire is carried to the far reaches of the Orthodox world.

THE PLACE CALLED

This skull-like hill outside the Damascus Gate of Old Jerusalem answers
the ruins presently thereon are those of a

GOLGOTHA

well the Biblical description of the place of Christ's crucifixion. Part of church dating from the time of the Crusades.

There is so much of jealousy and envy surrounding this great church that one finds relatively little inspiration in visiting it. Perhaps the most charitable judgment one can give is that attributed to Bishop Gore. When asked what he thought Jesus would say, he replied: "I believe he would say: 'My children must have toys. Do not all children sometimes quarrel about their toys?' "*

In contrast to the Church of the Holy Sepulcher is the garden tomb near what is known as Gordon's Calvary. In 1849 Otto Thenius suggested that a hill known as Jeremiah's Grotto to the north of the modern Damascus Gate might be the true site of the crucifixion. It is a rocky ridge, with shallow caves at one end, that bears a certain resemblance to a human skull. Fisher Howe in 1871 also supported Thenius' suggestion, and it found an earnest advocate in the person of the famous British general Charles George ("Chinese") Gordon. Nearby, at the base of the hill, Gordon found a large burial cave which, he believed, might well be the one in which Jesus was buried. The cave was in a garden; the tomb was large, a rich man's tomb, closed by a stone rolled in front of the door. The tomb had a small window at the entrance so that one looking in could see clearly by the light of this opening, as John peered into the tomb on Easter morn. Excavations in the garden revealed an old wine press and stones from a heathen temple. Those living near called this place "the hill of the skull."

Those who consider this cave to have been the true sepulcher cannot prove their belief, but as the place has been kept simple and unspoiled, one standing there on an Easter morning, as we did some years ago, finds a place appropriately hushed and commanding of reverence. One can readily imagine the anxious women gathering at the tomb and the angel voice saying to them: "He is not here, he is risen. Go, tell his disciples."

* Quoted in Morton, *op. cit.*, p. 61.

TOMB WHERE CHRIST WAS LAID

This ancient tomb, under the Hill of Golgotha, is thought by many to be the very one in which Jesus was laid. Before the tomb is a deep groove in which a great stone could have stood to close the entrance.

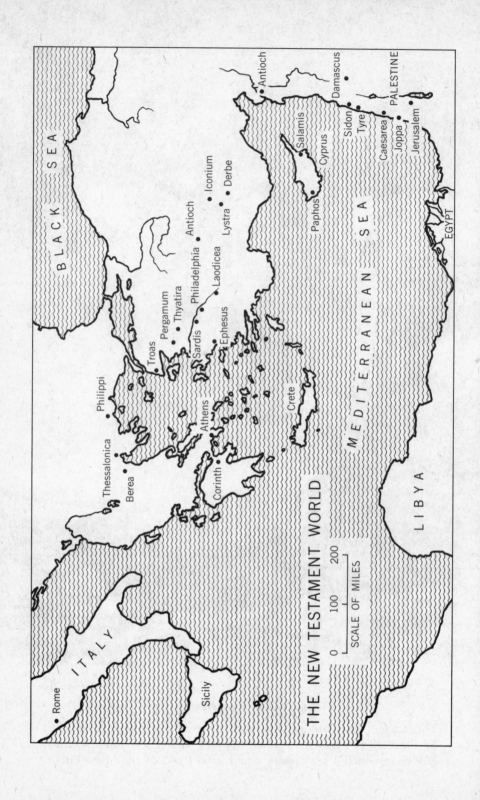

THE NEW TESTAMENT WORLD

SCALE OF MILES

0    100    200

# 18

# THE EXPANDING CHURCH

IN THE OPENING CHAPTERS OF THE BOOK OF ACTS, THE PEOPLE WHO belong to the Freedmen's synagogue are active in opposing the Christian movement. In view of the constant references to synagogues in the Gospels and Acts it seems strange to learn that no ruins have been found of first-century synagogues. But this can be accounted for: both Titus and Hadrian systematically destroyed Jewish synagogues. In 1920, a French archeologist, Raymond Weill, found in Jerusalem a stone inscribed with an account of the erection of a synagogue by one Theodotus, son of Vettinus, priest and chief of the synagogue. The name Vettini is that of a well-known patrician family. Since Theodotus took his name from the Roman family, the supposition is that he had once been their slave and later was freed and allowed to return to Palestine; he had retained the name of his old patron. In the Book of Acts we find reference to the Freedmen's synagogue, indicating that there was but one. It would appear reasonably certain that the inscription is from the very synagogue whose members attacked Saint Stephen.

After Jerusalem and Pentecost, the first important center of the Christian movement was the storied city of Damascus. Built on the edge of the great Syrian desert, it owes its greatness and persistence to its two rivers, the Abana and the Pharpar. One flows from the slopes of Mount Hermon on the southwest, the other comes from the anti-Lebanon mountains on the northwest. Both are clear and beautiful streams watering a broad stretch of the fertile plain and making possible the wonderful gardens of Damascus. Arabic poets compared Damascus and its gardens to the gardens of Paradise, and it is said of Mohammed that when his forces captured the city and he was invited to enter and view his conquest he refused, saying that he feared lest enjoying the beauties of her gardens would destroy in him the longing for the gardens of Paradise —a legend apt if apocryphal, since Damascus was captured by the Arabs only after Mohammed's death. It is today a beautiful city of white roofs and minarets and seductive green orchards, and is believed to be the oldest continuously inhabited city in the world. The name of Damascus appears again and again in Holy Writ from the earliest times, in connection with the story of Abraham, and down through the New Testament and the story of the conversion of Saul. During the period of the kings of Israel it was the capital of Syria and a bitter foe of Israel. Overrun in turn by the Assyrians, the Greeks and the Romans, it was in the time of Jesus a part of the kingdom of Aretas IV, who ruled from Petra, from 9 B.C. to A.D. 40. Herod Antipas married the daughter of Aretas IV and later divorced her in order to marry Herodias, his brother's wife, a deed that resulted in a war of revenge and a loss of some of Herod's territory. Saint Paul is our only authority for saying that Aretas was then king of Damascus, but confirmation for this statement is found in the coins of that day. The coins of Damascus bear the image of the Roman emperor Tiberius who ruled until A.D. 34. Thereafter the heads of the Roman emperors Caligula, ruling 37–41, and Claudius, 41–54, do not appear on Damascus coins. With Nero, ruling from A.D. 62, the heads of the Roman emperors again appear, showing that from 34 to 62 some other king—quite possibly Aretas IV— ruled Damascus.

The eastern gate of Damascus, standing today, is in part a relic of Roman times, and the straight street leading from it is called the Derb ul Mostaqim, or "the street which is called Straight," as mentioned in Acts 9:11. In the time of Saint Paul, this was one of the most famous thoroughfares of the ancient world, a mile long and a hundred feet wide, with colonnades on either side of the central roadway. The largest mosque in the modern city is a Christian cathedral transformed. It purports to contain the severed head of John the Baptist in the ornate shrine in the center of the building. Calvin records that in his day there were no less than twenty Christian churches that claimed to possess this same sacred relic; we may be pardoned a degree of skepticism as to the authenticity of the present claim. To the Christian the most moving feature of the mosque is an entablature over the bricked-up south doorway. The entablature, which can be seen by climbing to the top of a bazaar adjoining, bears what Henry Van Dyke has called the "bravest inscription" in the world. It reads: "Thy kingdom, O Christ, is a kingdom of all ages, and Thy dominion lasts throughout all generations."[*]

Another city outside Jerusalem closely linked with the early history of the Christian church is Caesarea. It was here that the Roman centurion Cornelius saw the vision of an angel bidding him to send to Joppa for a man named Peter. It was here Peter came in response to his request and to his heavenly vision of the sheet let down from Heaven. It was here that the Holy Spirit fell upon the Romans for the first time and Jews and Gentiles ate together. Following Paul's visit to Rome after his conversion and learning of a rumor of a plot to kill him, he left for his home in Tarsus by way of Caesarea. Here too was the home of Deacon Philip and his four prophetic daughters. Here Paul presented his defense to Felix and to Festus in company of Herod Agrippa and Bernice. And it was here that he terminated two years in prison by appealing to Caesar. The good physician Luke accompanied Paul on the journey and was with him on the voyage to Rome; it is reasonable to suppose that Luke used the two years of waiting to gather material for what later became the Gospel of Luke. So Caesarea, with good cause, figures prominently in the narrative of the Book of Acts.

Caesarea was a new city, erected by Herod the Great on a spot halfway between the Haifa and Joppa of today, on what had been a barren plain. It was truly one of Herod's triumphs. There was no harbor there; Herod set out at terrific expenditure of time and money to make one. Huge stones were brought from the mountains and dumped into the sea to make a circular breakwater, closed on the south and west and open only to the north, where ships might safely anchor.

The mole was two hundred feet wide, the harbor at some places one hundred and twenty feet deep. It took twelve years of prodigious labor to complete the project. On the shore nearby, Herod caused to be built a tall marble temple surmounted by statues of Roma and Augustus, clearly visible to ships far out at sea. Within the city he built a luxurious palace and made Caesarea his capital.

[*] Henry Van Dyke, *Out-of-Doors in The Holy Land* (New York: Chas. Scribner's Sons, 1908), p. 323.

After his death, successive Roman procurators used the palace as a residence, going to Jerusalem only at feast times when there was the danger of "incidents." With the progress of Christianity, Caesarea became in later days a strong Christian center and the bishop's residence. The most famous of its bishops was Eusebius, the great ecclesiastical historian.

Today one sees on the site of Caesarea miles of sand dunes strewn with chips of marble with weathered sandstone looking like petrified sponge. The ruins of the great harbor breakwater can be seen stretching out to sea. In many an Arab hut Roman pillars have become a part of the walls. A vault in what appears to be the crypt of a demolished cathedral is shown to visitors today as Paul's prison, and in it Greek Orthodox services are conducted. One can still see the great amphitheater seating twenty thousand persons and the arches of a ruined aqueduct. Farther inland another aqueduct carries an abundant supply of water. But there is little else to remind one that this was once a thriving city and the center of a great Christian movement.

In Acts 11:26 is related the manner in which the Christian church spread to the city of Antioch. It was at Antioch that believers were first called Christians. Indeed, after the fall of Jerusalem, Antioch became the strongest center of Christian influence in the Near East. It was from Antioch that relief was sent by Paul and Barnabas to the famine sufferers in Jerusalem. It was from Antioch that the two apostles set out on their missions and here they returned. Its greatness and strategic location on the Orontes River, twenty miles from the sea, where the river carves the only opening that exists between the Lebanon and Taurus mountains, gave it the name "The Queen of the East." It was founded by the Greek king Seleucus I in 301 b.c., who altogether founded nine cities called Seleucias, sixteen called Antioch and six called Laodicea, the last named for his mother. In Paul's time Antioch was comprised of four successive and adjacent cities, each with its own wall but all encompassed by a greater wall. Following its capture by the Romans, it was proclaimed a free city and made the capital of Syria. Successive Roman emperors beautified it with memorial fountains of extraordinary beauty. Herod the Great paved one of its broad streets in marble and erected colonnades along it. Another broad street, four miles long, was a great east–west artery bisecting the southern part of the city.

ANTIOCH, WHERE CHRISTIANITY GOT ITS NAME

Once one of the most magnificent cities in the Near East, it is now a small, dusty town with Moslem prayer towers. Not to be confused with Antioch in Pisidia, where Paul was persecuted.

In *Ben-Hur,* his classic story of the first century, General Lew Wallace offers a striking description of Antioch as it must have appeared in those days, as a traveler approaching the city describes it to fellow passengers:

"The river here runs to the west. . . . I remember when it washed the base of the walls. Now the whole river front is taken up with wharves and docks. Yonder to the south is Mount Cassius looking across to its brother Amanus in the north; and between them lies the plain of Antioch. Farther are the Black Mountains whence the Ducts of the Kings bring the purest water to wash the thirsty streets and the people. But the wall of the city there it is, the masterpiece of Xeraeus the master of mural architecture." (High, solid and with many bold angles it curved southwardly out of view.) "On the top there are 400 towers, each a reservoir of water. The structure on the farthest crest is the citadel, garrisoned all the year round by a Roman legion. Opposite it this way rises the temple of Jupiter, and under that the front of the legates residence—a palace full of offices, yet a fortress against which a mob would dash as harmlessly as a south wind. The bridge yonder marks the limit of navigation. Above the bridge begins the island upon which Calinicus built his new city with five great viaducts so solid time has made no impression upon them, nor floods, nor earthquakes."

Antioch in that day was considered the third city of the empire, eclipsed only by Rome and by Alexandria. It covered half again as much land as did imperial Rome. Morally its reputation was evil. Juvenal says that the superstitions and immorality of the east flowed from the Orontes to the Tiber. Indeed it is probable that no population in all history have been more wholly abandoned to vice than some of the old Greco-Roman cities. A prolific center for the vice of Antioch was the town of Daphne, four miles distant, the site of a beautiful temple to the Pythian Apollo. Because the temple gave asylum to criminals, it became the haunt of the outcasts of society. By the profligate rites associated with its worship it attracted the evil and the notorious.

After the capture of the holy city of Jerusalem, Titus the conqueror set up one of the two cherubims from the Holy of Holies over the Antioch gate. From the Epistle to the Galatians we know that Peter resided at Antioch for a time, and the bishop of Antioch was given third place of honor after Alexandria and Rome at the Church Council of Nicaea. St. Chrysostom estimated that by the end of the fourth century among a population of around a quarter of a million in Antioch, there were one hundred thousand Christians. During the period 252–380, no less than ten church assemblies were held there. It was the mother church of Gentile Christianity.

In 1932 an American-British-French expedition began excavations at Antioch. Because the present city is much smaller than the old, there were many promising sites easily accessible. The ancient walls were retraced and the acropolis located. The ruins of a huge circus were disclosed, one of the largest in the world, erected originally by the Romans in the first century and capable of seating two hundred thousand people. Many baths, villas and other buildings were uncovered, including a Christian church erected A.D. 384. Many sculptured pieces were found and numerous floor mosaics dating from the first to the sixth centuries, depicting with a wealth of detail incidents from Greco-Roman history and mythology and landscapes and hunting scenes of high artistic merit.

The most famous object to be uncovered at Antioch was not found by archeologists but by Arab diggers who, in 1910, uncovered a treasure that included the Antioch Chalice. They refused to tell exactly where they discovered it but said it was under the ruins of an ancient cathedral. In addition to the chalice, they found a cross, book covers of silver and other treasures. The chalice, a large container for a simpler goblet, is exquisitely carved with figures believed to represent Christ and the apostles. There are two pictures of Christ on opposite sides, one depicting him as a boy and the other as a man. Ten figures salute the two Christs with uplifted hands. At the right hand of the Saviour is a plate with five loaves and two fishes, and just beyond them a dove. Beneath the feet of Christ is a Roman eagle. A vine design is intertwined with the other figures. After ten years of study the archeologist Eisen brought out a beautifully illustrated book devoted wholly to a description of the Antioch Chalice. Eisen identifies the figures around the youthful Christ as being Matthew, Mark, Luke and John, with James the son of Zebedee, and those around the adult Christ as Peter, Paul, James, Jude and Andrew. These figures are scarcely two inches high, but each is individually characterized. On the basis of its shape, Eisen identifies the chalice as being from around A.D. 70. No other goblets of this peculiar, small-based type were fashioned later than the time of Tiberius, whose reign ended A.D. 34.

Thus Eisen concludes that the portraits may well be authentic. Christ is pictured as beardless, his face radiating dignity and sweetness. The style is typical of the Greek school, at which this artisan would have been considered one of the most accomplished. The engraved chalice was designed to be the holder of a simple chalice which is plain and has pieces chipped from it. Dr. Eisen hazards the belief that the inner chalice may be the Holy Grail itself, the cup from which Jesus and his disciples drank on the last night; impossible to prove, it is a fascinating supposition.

Inevitably a great controversy has developed as a result of this discovery, especially as to the date of the chalice. Dr. Barton considers that the ideas reflected in the figures and the decorations are more appropriate to the early second century, say 120–140. Dr. Cook of Cambridge says they are appropriate either to the Flavian period, 70–96, or perhaps to the time of Trajan, 98–116. Foakes Jackson considers it definitely a first-century work. Others would make it as late as the fifth century. However, Dr. Bacon has shown that similar art forms are to be found at Baalbak in the temples erected in the second century, and Dougherty has proved that the same were employed much earlier in the Orient. A fascinating imaginative reconstruction of the preparation of this remarkable vessel appears in the novel *The Silver Chalice* by Thomas Costain. The chalice itself may be seen today at The Cloisters in New York, where it is the most prized of all the wonderful examples of early Christian art housed in that beautiful museum.

Two unusually interesting ruined churches have been found in the vicinity of Antioch. One of these, a large church, is at Seleucia Pieria, the ancient seaport of Antioch from which Paul and Barnabas sailed. It was built about A.D. 480. The floor of the ambulatory was covered with an extraordinary collection of mosaics showing a veritable paradise of natural life including animals, birds, trees, flowers and bits of landscape. Among the animals are to be seen a giraffe, a zebra startled by a large crane, an "irritable elephant," ferocious lions, inquisitive horses, fleet gazelles, goats, a hyena and other beasts. The birds include an eagle flapping its wings, a gallinule scratching its head, peacocks, flamingos, cranes, ducks and geese. Old Testament figures include Daniel, Moses and the burning bush, Joseph and Saul. New Testament stories pictured are the Adoration of the Magi, the rich man and Lazarus, and the feeding of the five thousand.

THE SILVER CHALICE

The most famous object uncovered at Antioch was not discovered by archeologists, but by Arab diggers in 1910. It is a container for a simpler chalice and is exquisitely carved in the Greek style with figures believed to represent Christ and the Apostles.

Some forty miles northeast of Antioch are the striking ruins of the Church of Saint Simeon. Simeon was born in northern Syria about A.D. 390 and as an act of devotion spent the last thirty years of his life living on progressively higher pillars. The first pillar was six feet high, the last about sixty feet. He spent most of his days bowing rapidly in prayer. One spectator began counting his prostrations and reached a total of 1,244 before he tired of counting—but Saint Simeon did not tire so easily. He is reputed to have stood on one leg for a year in a state of trance. From every quarter pilgrims by the thousand thronged to see him and thousands are reported to have been converted at the sight. A brilliant star is said to have shone over his pillar, a crowd of prelates followed him to his grave. He became a model of sainthood. Around his pillar, shortly after his death, a great church was erected, the impressive ruins of which still stand. Four rectangular halls were built in the shape of a cross. The Syrian historian Evagrius, who visited the church A.D. 560, wrote: "Handsome columns of polished stone sustain a roof of considerable elevation. The center is occupied by a court where stands the pillar of forty cubits on which the incarnate angel on earth spent his heavenly life." Monasteries were grouped around the church, and the ruins of the town show what elaborate preparations were necessary to accommodate the pilgrims who for centuries came to visit this place made memorable by him whom Evagrius called the aerial martyr.

# 19

# THE PATHWAYS
# OF ST. PAUL

IN ACTS 13:4–5, PAUL AND BARNABAS, STARTING ON THEIR FIRST
missionary journey, sailed for Cyprus, the home of Barnabas. Cyprus is a long, beautiful and fertile island in the eastern Mediterranean near enough to the Bay of Antioch to be visible from shore
on a clear day. It is about one hundred and fifty miles long and
fifty miles wide at its widest point. The first written record of the
history of Cyprus tells how the island was conquered by King
Thutmose III of Egypt, perhaps the first empire builder, about
1500 B.C. But long before his coming Cyprus was of great importance as one of the main sources of copper during the Bronze Age.
In ancient times Cyprians made objects of pure copper and did not
have to depend on imports of any kind. Between 3000–1200 B.C.,
the island flourished, with a large population and a considerable
foreign trade. There were large forests and diamond, emerald,
iron, lead, zinc and silver mines. The inhabitants possessed a
large fleet; indeed, it was the boast of Cyprians that they were
able to build their vessels unaided. The advent of the Iron Age
brought about the eclipse and decline of this ancient civilization.

Cyprus was a part of the great Persian empire of Darius and remained so until the defeat of the Persians at the battle of Issus in
333 B.C. The Cyprians, who by then had a large Greek element,
gladly threw in their lot with Alexander. The arrival of the Cyprian fleet during the siege of Tyre enabled Alexander to capture
that stronghold. About 58 B.C. the island was wrested from the
Greeks by the rising might of Rome and made a separate province.

The first Jews, according to Josephus, came to Cyprus shortly after, about 50 B.C.

Early in the second century, the Jews of Cyprus rose against Roman rule, massacred a quarter of a million inhabitants and destroyed a large part of Salamis. Hadrian, who later became emperor, suppressed the revolt and banished all Jews from Cyprus.

The Bible mentions two missionary visits to the island of Cyprus, the first by Paul, Mark and Barnabas, the second by Barnabas and Mark. They went first to Salamis, then one of the most important ports on the Mediterranean and the commercial capital of the island. In Paul's time there were several synagogues at Salamis, proof of a sizable Jewish community. Today, at a monastery named for him, one is shown the supposed tomb of Barnabas. The monks have a legend that on his second trip to the island, in the company of Mark, Barnabas was stoned to death in the hippodrome by a mob roused against him. Mark contrived to steal the body and buried it outside the city in a location kept secret. Four hundred years later the church in Cyprus strove to become independent of the see of Antioch by claiming that it was of equal importance because it, too, had been founded by an apostle. The dispute went against the Cyprian church until the archbishop announced that Saint Barnabas had appeared in a dream and revealed to him the location of the hidden grave. Further, Barnabas directed him to appeal to the Emperor Zeno at Constantinople. The next day the archbishop, with a crowd of followers, went to the place indicated and found the body of Barnabas with a copy of the Gospel of Matthew on his breast. The archbishop took the relics to the emperor, who was so impressed that he at once called a special meeting of the Synod which ended the dispute by granting independence to Cyprus. In addition, they gave the archbishop the right to sign his name in red ink, a privilege previously reserved to the emperor, and he was authorized to wear a purple cape and to carry a scepter instead of the customary staff. Today, after 1,450 years, these rights are still jealously preserved.

A dense wood covers the site of Salamis. Among the trees the stumps of marble pillars can be seen and the remains of three market places. There are enormous squares paved with marble; at one time they were surrounded by splendid buildings, now in ruins. Roman houses, with many bathrooms, each house with a complete system of central heating, have been found. In the largest forum

SITE OF THE CITY OF SALAMIS

The Bible mentions two missionary visits to the Island of Cyprus. Paul, Mark and Barnabas went first to Salamis, then one of the most important ports on the Mediterranean and the commercial center of the island. Today one sees woods and wilderness with stumps of marble pillars and the remains of three market places.

one can mount steps almost certainly trod by the apostles. The destruction of the city and the port was caused by a violent earthquake.

In the center of the island are great copper mines leased by Herod the Great from the Emperor Augustus. Our word *copper* comes from the name Cyprus. Today an American company using modern methods is working the old mines.

The apostles went from Salamis to Paphos, the residence of the Roman ruler. Near Paphos is a village called Salamiou surrounded by olive trees said to have grown from seeds tossed aside by Paul and Barnabas when they stopped there to rest and eat. Near Tamassos is a grave believed to be that of Mnason, the old disciple mentioned in the Book of Acts, 21:16. Mnason, believed to have been baptized by Saint John, lived one day's journey from Jerusalem, welcomed Paul and Luke and is said to have once performed a miracle, paralyzing the arm of an oppressive moneylender.

In Paphos the missionaries came in touch with the proconsul Sergius Paulus, a man of intelligence whose predecessor was the famous orator Cicero. In those days there were two classifications of Roman provinces. Some were under the rule of the Senate and ruled by a proconsul. Others were directly under the emperor and ruled by a procurator. Luke designates Pilate, Felix and Festus as procurators and Paulus as a proconsul. At one time Luke was thought to have erred in so naming Sergius Paulus as proconsul; it was known that the Emperor Augustus had retained Cyprus under his own control and thus would have been represented by a procurator. At a later time, however, Cyprus came again under the authority of the Senate. A coin bearing the inscription of a Cyprian proconsul has been found, and in recent years archeologists have unearthed an inscription written A.D. 55 and reading "In the time of the proconsul Paulus." Pliny also mentions Paulus as the author of a treatise on Cyprian lore. The presence and the office of this man have been abundantly confirmed.

It was at Paphos in the presence of Sergius Paulus that the dramatic contest between the magician Bar Jesus, or Elymas, and the apostle Paul occurred, a struggle that resulted in the blindness of Bar Jesus and the acceptance of the message of the missionaries by the proconsul. From the time of Paul's visit to Cyprus he no longer used the Hebrew form of his name, Saul, but the Latin, Paul. And though the mission to Cyprus began with Barnabas, mentioned first and apparently the leader, the group was later referred to as "Paul and his company" as the younger man took the lead. It is probable that moving out into the Roman world, the apostle found it to his advantage to use the Latin of his name rather than the Hebrew.

Leaving Cyprus, they returned to the mainland, making their first stop at the city of Antioch in Pamphylia, one of the sixteen Antiochs built by Seleucus I. The remains of its Roman aqueduct are still standing. Its principal temple, sacred to a god named Men, contained a great altar with many engraved tablets. In the underlying soil a quantity of animal bones has been found, suggesting ritual sacrifice. The city had two fine squares, one named for Augustus Caesar, the other for Tiberius, with archways adorned with relief carvings. The temple to Men has a wonderful frieze of carved bulls' heads joined by garlands of leaves and fruits, the bull's head being the symbol of Men, a god of fertility.

The city was an outstanding example of Grecian refinement and Roman luxury. Water brought to the city by the aqueduct was distributed through terra-cotta pipes. Found in the ruins was an edict in Latin forbidding profiteering and setting a price ceiling on grain after a severe winter. Antioch was first identified by one Francis Arundell, a British chaplain from Smyrna, whose interest in archeology was aroused by his brother-in-law James Morier, famous in Iran as the author of *Hajji Baba of Isfahan*. In Antioch, as was his custom, Paul entered the Jewish synagogue on the Sabbath day with his Gospel message. Apparently the Jewish colony was not large and there was but one synagogue. It would be much like the synagogue of today, with a reading desk in the center, a closed ark on the side nearest Jerusalem containing manuscripts of the Old Testament, seats on all sides so that all eyes were fixed on the reader, and a separate section for women, behind a lattice or in a gallery. Luke gives a fairly detailed account of Paul's sermon. It was conciliatory, commencing with the Old Testament prophecies and going on to the teachings of John and Jesus. The reception given Paul was friendly, but by the second week opposition appeared, and Paul made a dramatic announcement: "We turn to the Gentiles." It was an historic turning point and thereafter he became in fact as he was in his calling, the apostle to the Gentiles. In so strongly romanized a city, a Roman colony, any appeal before the law against the apostles would have been fruitless. Hence

Paul's enemies sought to stir up certain influential women, devout proselytes to Judaism. The apostles were forced to move on to Iconium, or Konium as it is known today, six miles distant.

Near Iconium are two hills known as the hills of Paul and Thecla. Thecla was a young convert from Iconium, whose history is related in the Apocryphal Acts of Paul and Thecla, a work widely read by members of the early church. It contains the only description of Paul's physical appearance that survives: "A man of little stature, thin-haired upon the head, crooked in the legs, of good state of body, with eyebrows joining, and nose somewhat hooked, full of grace; for sometimes he appeared like a man, and sometimes he had the face of an angel."

Iconium was not a Roman colony but a democratic Greek city. The apostles were assaulted by a mob and fled to Lystra. Little if anything of the city Paul saw has remained. The old city was repeatedly destroyed and rebuilt.

The site of Lystra, twenty-five miles from Iconium, was discovered by an American professor, J. R. Stillington Sterrett, in 1885. An altar stone three and one-half feet high was unearthed, the name of the city carved on it in Latin, indicating that Lystra was a Roman colony. Since the altar dates from the time of Augustus, Paul and his companions doubtless saw it. It was here that Paul's healing of the lame man led the priest of Jupiter to sacrifice to him as to a god. The people hailed Barnabas and Paul as the earthly forms of Jupiter and Mercury. It is easy to understand why these identifications were made in Lystra, for it was here that the story of Philemon and Baucis had its origin. The tradition has it that Jupiter and Mercury came in human form to visit the city and were driven out by the inhospitable villagers; only Philemon and his wife Baucis were ready to welcome them. In a miraculous way Philemon's limited supply of food was doubled to accommodate his guests. The following day a lake was discovered where the city had been and the cruel villagers had been turned into fish. It was inevitable that when people of Lystra believed two gods had come among them, they would think of Jupiter and Mercury. Furthermore, it appears that these gods were the patrons of the city. Excavation has uncovered the ruins of a temple and an inscription to "Zeus before the city," as described in the Book of Acts, and many votary tablets have been found dedicated to the gods Jupiter (or Zeus) and Mercury. The great excitement of the priest of Jupiter is easy to understand, as is his concern that the reception of the gods would be such as to merit blessing and not disaster.

The final stop on Paul's tour, the city of Derbe, has not been certainly identified. All four of these cities, Antioch, Iconium, Lystra and Derbe, were included in the Roman province of Galatia in Roman times. There is good reason to believe that Paul's Epistle to the Galatians was addressed to the Christians of the province. The district had been settled by the Gauls in 278 B.C. and became a Roman colony in 64 B.C. From there the apostles retraced their steps to the coast and returned to their original base of Antioch in Syria.

On the second missionary journey, after visiting many of the cities touched on the first tour, Paul and Silas went to Troas in western Asia Minor. There Paul's vision of the man of Macedonia pleading for help was taken as a sign from God that the apostles were to go on to Europe. They had added Timothy to their number in Lystra and joined Luke in Troas, so apparently there were four who embarked on this historic mission. It is instructive to contrast their journey to Europe and the invasion organized by the Persian king, Xerxes, which began from almost the same spot in 480 B.C., some five hundred years before. Xerxes' expedition was the mightiest force of which ancient history bears record. Herodotus has given a vivid and fascinating picture of the great host gathered from all parts of the Persian Empire. From India to Abyssinia, from Arabia to Afghanistan they gathered, some on foot and some on horseback, armed with swords, spears, wearing bronze helmets, helmets of horses' skulls and an amazing variety of dress and uniform. Herodotus says that so many were gathered together that it was necessary to single out ten thousand and build an enclosure around them. The enclosure was used as a measuring unit and the waiting troops were led in to estimate the total number on hand. It was estimated that in the army of Xerxes there was a grand total of 1,700,000 men. In addition to this mighty host, 1,207 ships were anchored in the Hellespont and prepared to do battle. Seated on his marble throne, Xerxes looked out upon the sea of soldiery and announced that he was at last a happy man. The signal to advance was given and under the whips of the officers the army began to move across a great bridge of boats to the far side.

The result of this mighty effort is a matter of history. We know that the Persians met fierce resistance from the Greeks, their vast navy was defeated at sea and their armies scattered on land. Only a pitiful remnant of Xerxes' apparently invincible army escaped. Contrast this with Paul's undertaking. Four men starting out to conquer a continent! Four unknown, unarmed, impoverished evangelists, desiring to do what Xerxes never dreamed of doing, changing the hearts, the characters, the lives and the religion of the people of Greece, of the Western world. Xerxes would have been satisfied with outer submission and the payment of taxes and indemnities. Paul and his companions would be satisfied with nothing less than total surrender, body, mind and spirit. Yet the incredible marvel is that Paul succeeded where Xerxes failed. He launched a movement that in time won not only Greece but the continent of Europe.

Philippi, the first city in Europe at which they stopped to preach, was named for Philip of Macedon, who founded the city in the fourth century B.C. In later days it was famous as the site of the Battle of Philippi at which Antony and Octavian defeated Cassius and Brutus. In celebration of the victory in 42 B.C., the city was made a Roman colony and the veterans of the battle became its outstanding citizens. Paul's party landed at Neapolis, nine miles distant, from which one of the most famous highways of the time, the Via Egnatia, passing through the center of Philippi, led across Greece and on to Rome. The way has been uncovered at various places and one can still see ruts three and four inches deep worn by the passing of the wheels of countless chariots.

The French school of Athens carried out extensive excavations at Philippi from 1914 to 1938. In the center of the old city was found a forum three hundred feet long and half as wide, with a temple at either end, five porticoes on three sides and many public buildings surrounding it. On the north side was a high podium from which the ruler dispensed justice, as told in the Book of Acts 16:19. In another section was an acropolis, a theater and churches of a much later date than Paul's time. The ruins of a colonial archway were found at the west end of the old city. Evidently dating from Roman times, it was probably built when Philippi was made a colony and very probably marks the end of the pomerium beyond which foreigners were forbidden to pass. About a mile from the city one comes to the Gangites River, mentioned in Acts 16:13, where Paul and the apostles found a group of devout women worshiping on the Sabbath. One of these was Lydia, the dealer in purple, who became their first European convert. The Gangites is a clear, shallow stream, ten to twelve yards wide. The city was a military center in the days of Paul. It was at Philippi that the clairvoyant girl was healed, the apostles beaten and imprisoned, where the earthquake struck by night and the jailer was converted. Paul's warm feeling for the Christians of this place is communicated in his letter to the Philippians, unique among his letters to the churches he visited in that it contains no words of criticism or warning.

The apostles went on to Thessalonica, seven miles distant along the Via Egnatia. Founded by Cassander about 315 B.C., it was named for his wife, a sister of Alexander the Great. At the time of the battle of Philippi the city sided with the victors and was rewarded by being made a free city. Its main street followed the Via Egnatia. A ruined gate, called the Vardar gate, has been found bearing the words "in the time of the Politarchs." In the Greek translation of Acts 17:6 we find the rulers of the city referred to as politarchs, which at one time gave rise to criticism of the Book of Luke for using a title unknown to history. Several inscriptions using the term politarchs, from the time of Augustus, have been found in Thessalonica; once again, Luke has been proved to be accurate. It was in Thessalonica that the apostles were accused of being "those who have turned the world upside down," something that very much needed doing.

Not long after leaving Thessalonica, Paul entered the great city of Athens, the world's center of philosophy, art and architecture. Did he wonder if, in the light of their splendid achievement, the Athenians would not be content with their own ways of worship? The city contains some of the most beautiful objects made by man. Many writers and travelers described its glories. In 1841 W. M. Leake began the first modern excavations on the site of old Athens. At present six foreign schools co-operate with the Greek government in large-scale excavations of the ruins. The center of the ancient city was the Acropolis, a soaring rock some five hundred and twelve feet high, which has been a gathering place since neolithic times. Athens emerged from obscurity in the seventh century B.C. and rose to the leadership of the Greek states during the Persian wars. Under Pericles in 443–429 the city enjoyed its golden age. Inspired by Phidias the sculptor, Athens was arrayed with a wonderful profusion of temples, public buildings and works of art.

THE RUINS

Called the birthplace of Christianity in Europe, it was here
was here too that Lydia, the wealthy

*Religious News Service Photo*

OF PHILIPPI

in Greece that Paul preached his first sermon to the Gentiles. It
woman, became the first convert in Europe.

From the spoils of the victory of Marathon, Phidias made a colossal bronze statue of Athena and placed it on the Acropolis. Mariners rounding the promontory of Dunius could see the sun flashing from Athena's spear and helmet. Another image of Athena, with the glorius Parthenon to house it, was erected. Athena's statute was made of wood and covered with ivory; the face and hands were of ivory, the eyes of jewels, her tresses and helmet of gold. Mahaffy has written: "There is no ruin all the world over which combines so much striking beauty, so distinct a type, so vast a volume of history, so great a pageant of immortal memories. . . . All the Old World's culture culminated in Greece—all Greece in Athens—all Athens in its Acropolis—all the Acropolis in the Parthenon."* A commentary on the morality of the times is the precaution taken by Phidias; he ordered that the statue of Athena be made in such a way that the precious ornamentation might be removed and weighed when, as he foresaw, he was accused of misappropriation.

In Paul's time images were everywhere. Immediately inside the Piraeus gate were statues of Minerva, Jupiter, Apollo, Mercury and the Muses, and nearby a sanctuary to Bacchus. There were altars erected to Fame, to Modesty, to Energy, to Persuasion and to Pity. On the Acropolis itself, in addition to the statues mentioned, were groups representing Theseus wrestling the Minotaur, the infant Hercules in the act of strangling the serpents, Minerva causing the olive to sprout and Neptune rising from the waves. No wonder, as Luke tells us, "his spirit was provoked within him as he saw that the city was full of idols." It was easier, as one satirist expressed it, to find an idol in Athens than a man.

The worship of idols was not an impetus to holy living. It brought the worshiper no closer to God and gave him no longing for righteousness. Indeed, the gods themselves were no better than men. They had only two claims to superiority—they were more powerful and they were immortal. But they lied and committed adultery and were unjust, partisan, unscrupulous and capricious. As the philosopher Seneca observed, "No other effect can possibly be produced than that all shame for sin be taken away from men who believe in such gods."

No wonder then that Paul, the warrior of righteousness, was stirred to the depths as he looked on a teeming throng devoted to the worship of false gods.

* Quoted in Finegan, *op. cit.*, p. 273.

Second to the Acropolis was the agora, or market place, center of the city's cultural and commercial life. Luke comments on the eager curiosity of the Athenians of his day in Acts 17:21, an observation seconded by other ancient writers. It was here, Luke tells us, that Paul disputed with the Jews and other devout persons who met with them. The American School of Classical Studies has removed nearly a quarter of a million tons of earth from the agora, uncovering large sections of it. Investigations reveal that the agora was surrounded with a marvelous assembly of strikingly beautiful buildings—colonnaded porticoes, a temple to Apollo Patros, the Bouleterion where the Council of Five Hundred met, the circular Thelos of the Executive Council, the temple of Ares, a music hall and a library. It was in such surroundings that Paul commenced his ministry to the Athenians.

It was not long before the local teachers of philosophy heard of the strange new teaching brought to Athens by an itinerant Jew. They demanded an explanation. Some inquired: "What would this babbler say?" The word *babbler* means seed picker or scavenger. It might be translated as *wit scavenger*—this man who has picked up stray bits of philosophical refuse from the streets of the world. They had Paul brought to the Areopagus.

Originally the word Areopagus referred to a court which gathered on Mars Hill west of the Acropolis. The hill is of bare rock and is three hundred and seventy-seven feet high. Near the top, some fifteen or sixteen steps cut from solid rock led to the summit on which was a smooth platform with stone benches on three sides. Here the city fathers met to constitute the supreme assembly which had power in both political and religious affairs. By Paul's time, however, the court had transferred its meeting place to a building known as the Royal Stoa at one side of the agora; it is possible that this was the location of Paul's famous speech.

It was not the first time Paul had met with Greek philosophers, for his native city of Tarsus was famous as a city of philosophers, especially of the Stoic philosophers. Two of the most famous of the second generation of Stoic philosophers were Antipater of Tarsus and Zeno of Tarsus. Undoubtedly Paul was familiar with their logic and methods of thought. That his approach was effective is evidenced by the fact that one of his converts in Athens was an Areopagite, a member of the supreme tribunal before which he made his defense. Paul's speech here differed markedly from his address to the Jews in Antioch. He made no reference to the Old Testament, which would have been meaningless to them, but to Greek poetry and philosophy and to local altars and temples. To hear Paul speak of an altar "to an unknown god" seems incredible to us. But it is fully confirmed by other writers, who mention altars to unknown gods. Apollonius of Tyana, who visited Athens about the time Paul did, thought it a proof of wisdom "to speak well of all the gods, especially at Athens, where altars are set up in honor even of unknown gods.° A geographer named Pausanius visited Athens in the middle of the second century and noted that on the road from the harbor to the city he had seen "altars of the gods named Unknown" and an altar of "Unknown Gods" at Olympia.† Recently, at Pergamum, an inscription has been found which reads: "To unknown gods, Capito, torch-bearer."

Paul's stay in Athens was short and few converts were made. Regarding one convert, Dionysius the Areopagite, there are several interesting tales. It is said that he afterward stayed with Paul in Rome and was with him until the time of Paul's martyrdom. Later he was sent as a missionary to Gaul by Clement of Rome. He settled on an island in the Seine, made many converts and became bishop of Paris. During the Domitian persecution, he is said to have suffered martyrdom on Martyr Hill, or Montmartre as we know it. Canonized as a saint, he is known as Saint Dionysius, Saint Denys, the patron saint of France.

It is probably true that in Athens there are more buildings standing which Paul saw than in all the rest of the ancient world. The museums in Athens contain a plethora of ancient relics of rare beauty, gold head coverings, coins, statuary and jewels.

When Paul and the apostles journeyed on to Corinth, they approached the commercial capital of Greece. Timothy and Silas joined Paul and shared in his work at Corinth. The city is on the west side of the narrow isthmus that connects the Peleponnesus with the mainland. Almost opposite on the east was the port of Cenchreae, less than ten miles away. Ships from the east came to Cenchreae and ships from Spain, Sicily and Rome to Lechaeum, the port of Corinth. Small ships were hauled bodily across the isthmus from one port to the other; larger ships were unloaded and their cargoes transferred by pack animals and carts. In this way the

° Quoted in Finegan, *op. cit.*, p. 276.
† *Ibid.*

long detour around Cape Malea was avoided, a two hundred-mile trip made dangerous by winds and currents and rocky shoals. Strabo wrote: "When you double Malea forget your home." As early as the time of Alexander the Great the construction of a canal through the isthmus was considered and proposed. It was begun A.D. 66, when the Emperor Nero broke ground with a golden spade. Six thousand Jews captured by Vespasian in the Jewish war were put to work on the project. But Nero was dissuaded from continuing by an adviser who convinced him that the western sea was higher and such a canal would inundate valuable land. The work was abandoned and only finished in modern times, from 1881 to 1893. The modern canal is four miles long and is crossed by a high bridge.

Drawing commerce from east and west, Corinth flourished. By 600 B.C. it was one of the great centers of trade, and Corinthian potteries and bronzes have been found all around the Mediterranean. Disaster came to the city in 146 B.C. when, defeated in a war with Rome, it was completely destroyed and its inhabitants sold into slavery. One hundred years later, in 46 B.C., Julius Caesar rebuilt the city and caused it to be settled by Italians and displaced Greeks. It grew rapidly and was made the head of the provincial government by Augustus and the seat of the proconsul, as noted in Acts 18:12. In the fifteenth century it was captured by the Turks. It is an agricultural district rich in grapes; our word *currant* comes from Corinth. Twice in modern times, in 1858 and again in 1928, the city was devastated by earthquake.

Beginning in 1896, the American School of Classical Studies has carried on excavations at Corinth. The old city was found to have been built on two terraces, one a hundred feet higher than the other. Behind the city is a towering mountain, the Acrocorinth. The city in the time of Paul was about six miles in circumference, surrounded by walls, and with a double wall two miles long and forty feet high extending to the port of Lechaeum. A stately gateway on the north surmounted the Lechaeum road. Northwest of the agora was a temple to Apollo, dating from 600 B.C.: seven fine Doric columns still stand. On the Acrocorinth was the infamous temple to Aphrodite, served by a thousand priestesses, but of this so far no trace has been found. Beneath the shops on the agora archeologists uncovered an underground water system, carrying water for drinking and serving as a cooling system. An inscription calls one of the shops a shambles, the same designation used in I Corinthians

10:25 to describe a butcher's stall. Another inscription refers to a man called Erastus, recording that a pavement was constructed by him as "commissioner of public works." Can he be the Erastus mentioned in Acts 19:22 and Romans 16:23? It may be; he is referred to as the chamberlain of the city, a man of importance. In 1898, a stone found near the Lechaeum road was inscribed "Synagogue of the Jews," and was estimated to have been cut between 100 B.C. and A.D. 200. The rather crude writing betokens an ill-educated congregation. It may well have been over the door of the chapel where Paul preached. In I Corinthians 1:26, Paul confesses that "not many mighty" have been converted.

In excavating the agora it was found that one of its prominent features was an elevated platform, described as the rostra, the Latin equivalent of a Greek word used by Luke to describe the rostrum where Gallio sat during the hearings described in Acts 18:12–17. There can be little doubt that this is the spot where Paul stood before Gallio.

As to Gallio himself, he is known to history as a brother of the philosopher Seneca, and he is mentioned by both Tacitus and Dio Cassius. An inscription has been found across the Gulf of Corinth and six miles inland dated in the twenty-sixth year of Claudius, A.D. 52, in which the writer refers to a report that had reached him "from my friend Lucius Junius Gallio, the proconsul of Achaia." This inscription not only confirms the presence of Gallio and his title as proconsul, but very nearly fixes the date of Paul's arrival in Corinth. Paul had been in Corinth one and one-half years before Gallio arrived; Gallio would have been in Corinth some months before preparing the report referred to in the inscription. It would follow that Paul must have arrived in Corinth about A.D. 50.

The new city of Corinth had no aristocracy other than that of wealth. It grew rapidly and the city became notorious as a home of vice and drunkenness. In the plays of the time the drunken actor was always a Corinthian and to "Corinthianize" was a synonym for degrading. I Corinthians 6:9–11 reveals that the infant church was salvaged from just such people. The epistle indicates that the members of the church were loose, quarrelsome, boastful men, given to ecstatic faiths. It was here that Paul was joined by Prisca and Aquilla who, with other Jews, had been expelled from Rome by Claudius. Suetonius confirms this event, saying Claudius did so because the Jews "were always rioting through some agitator named Chrestus," in reference, no doubt, to attacks on the new Christians. Here the three, Paul, Prisca and Aquilla, worked at their trade, that of tentmaking and the making of sails. Such a center of commerce was an ideal place in which to ply their trade.

Another feature of life in old Corinth was the biennial celebration of the Isthmian games, one of four famous spectacles. The Olympian games were the more celebrated. Such was the excitement engendered by these games that they have been called a passion rather than a recreation. Since Paul spent two years in Corinth he almost certainly witnessed one of these thrilling contests. His letters to the Corinthians contain many figures of speech drawn from the games. The passage, I Corinthians 9:24–27, for example, uses figuratively the race, the prize, training rules, the victor's crown, the boxer. There are references to the race course, the judge, the herald and fighting with beasts. In that connection we are told that all athletes who wished to compete had to take an oath to abide by strict training rules for a period of ten months before the games. We see that, in every way, the account in the Book of Acts and references in the Epistles conform to the life of old Corinth as archeologists have reconstructed it.

Paul's visit to Corinth for another reason marks an important milestone in Christian history, for it is from Corinth that he wrote what was presumably the first document to be included in the collection that became known as the New Testament. Because the Gospels appear first in our New Testament, we naturally suppose that they are the oldest and the first to be composed. In fact, Paul's first letter to the Thessalonians, written from Corinth, antedates the earliest Gospel, that of Mark, by fifteen or twenty years. This fact is significant in tracing the course of Christian theology. Many readers have supposed they could see how Christian theology developed—the Gospel of Mark, the oldest, reflecting the humanity of Christ with little about his deity, the much later Gospel of John emphasizing the deity of Christ. They believed that the doctrine of Christ's deity is the result of a long process of evolution running over a century. However, in the earliest letters, written long before Mark's Gospel, we have a fully developed Christology with an explicit statement of the doctrine embodied in the Gospel of John. Jesus is One in whom the believers and the church exist, the Son from Heaven who was raised from the dead and will come again, the living source of grace and comfort.

Paul wrote many letters to the church of Corinth. We have two of them in the New Testament, with the possibility that a third is included in what we know as II Corinthians 10–13. The letter of I Corinthians is obviously not the first Paul wrote to that church; he refers in it to a previous letter.

In I Corinthians we have reflected the scandals that had broken out in that little Christian community—factionalism, immorality, drunkenness, oppression—scandals that are not surprising when we remember the evil environment in which the Christians of Corinth lived. But the marvel of it is that God's loyal servant Paul "used" these same scandals to bring incalculable blessings to people everywhere. Because of evidence of factionalism, Paul was inspired to teach of the church as the body of Christ. Because some taught that the resurrection was already past, we have Paul's triumphant declaration of faith in the coming resurrection. Because of their lack of love and lack of concern for other values, we have the marvelous psalm of love contained in the thirteenth chapter of I Corinthians. How amazing is the divine alchemy, that Paul could use the temporary yet distressing evils of the church at Corinth to enrich and bless all of God's churches to the end of time!

Of the places Paul visited on his recorded missionary journeys, he remained longest at Ephesus, some three years. The city had a long history, having been founded many centuries before Paul appeared and been captured successively by Croesus, Cyrus, Alexander and the Romans. At an undetermined time it became the capital of the province, and in Paul's day it ranked with Antioch and Alexandria as one of the three largest cities in the eastern empire. It is located on the left bank of the Cayster River three miles from the sea. In Paul's time it was a sea harbor, though the river required frequent dredging to keep it open for ships. The nearest railway station to the site today is Ayasaluke, a contraction of *Agios Theologos,* a title applied to the Apostle John, who is reputed to have spent his last years at Ephesus. Justinian the emperor erected a fine church to the memory of Saint John.

Ephesus was especially famed as a center of the worship of Artemis. Originally she was a local goddess, but she was adopted by the Greeks and identified with their own deity Artemis or Diana. In 1863 an English architect, J. T. Wood, began explorations on the abandoned site of the city, principally in the hope of recovering the site of Diana's temple. He had six years of discouraging failure, harassed by mosquitoes, curious visitors and the Turks. But after six years he found an inscription that gave him a lead. It described a number of gold and silver images, weighing six or seven pounds apiece, presented to the goddess and to be kept in her temple. An endowment was established for cleaning and caring for the images, and directions given that on the birthday of the goddess these images were to be carried in solemn procession to the theater, entering the city by the Magnesian gate and returning by the Corissian gate. By following the road which linked these gates, Wood was rewarded—he found in 1877 the ruins of the temple to Diana over a mile northwest of the city proper.

Later excavations by British and Austrians have produced impressive results. In the sixth century B.C. the original temple was a simple shrine with a wooden image. Successive temples were built on the same location, the one dedicated in 430 B.C. having taken a hundred and twenty years to build. It burned, and a Greek temple was begun about 350 B.C., its completion encouraged by Alexander. This was one hundred and sixty-three feet wide and three hundred and forty-two feet long. There were about one hundred marble columns over fifty-five feet high supporting its roof. The roof was covered with large marble slabs adorned with sculpture and gold. One ancient traveler reports: "I have seen the walls and hanging gardens of old Babylon, the statue of Olympian Jove, the Colossus of Rhodes, the great labour of the lofty pyramids, the ancient tomb of Mausolus. But when I beheld the temple of Ephesus towering to the clouds, all these other marvels were eclipsed." Truly it deserved the acclaim: *Great is Diana of the Ephesians.*

The statue of Diana in the temple was believed to have fallen from heaven; this so-called "sacred stone" was undoubtedly a meteorite. Each year the city observed a month of pilgrimage when ordinary business was suspended. There was a daily program that included athletic contests, plays and a religious procession. Thousands of silver shrines were sold to pilgrims as souvenirs. On the festival days a great statue of Diana was hauled through the streets on a cart drawn by mules, stags and fauns. Under the altar of the temple, excavators found thousands of gold and electrum objects, including statues of Diana. The temple was clearly identified by the discovery of its famous drums, richly sculptured, donated by King Croesus of Lydia, which are now on display in London.

The city of Ephesus was proud of its distinction as the guardian of Diana's temple, and was proud of the title "Necorus," literally "temple sweeper," which is translated as "temple keeper" in the Book of Acts. The title is found repeatedly on the old coins of Ephesus. Records reveal that the official called the town clerk, who used the phrase in the Book of Acts, was a man of outstanding prestige and influence. He was the keeper of the state archives, read important communications before the senate and assembly and was present when money was deposited. Letters sent to the people of Ephesus were addressed to him. He had the authority and presence to calm the mob as we find him doing when rioting silversmiths upset the town, and he warned the people of the possible consequences of such turbulence. The Asiarchs, who presided over games and religious rites and are mentioned as being friends of Paul and warned him against appearing in public during the riots, were other outstanding men of whom we have record. Each spring every principal town of the district selected one of its most wealthy and influential citizens as a candidate for this office. From among these candidates ten men were chosen as Asiarchs. It was necessary that they should be men of wealth, as they were expected to spend large sums meeting the expenses of the annual games. The fact that Paul numbered some of these prominent men among his friends indicates to what an extent his message had permeated the city.

Here Paul worked and preached, as he relates in Acts 20:31. In the afternoon he taught in the school of Tyrannus and was rewarded with success, so great, in fact, that magical books to the value of fifty thousand pieces of silver were voluntarily brought in and burned. So great was the loss of business to the image sellers because of Paul's work that they raised a riot against him and a great mob poured into the theater shouting praises to Diana. The theater is situated on a hill overlooking the city, the hollow of the hill forming a natural amphitheater capable of accommodating twenty-five thousand. It had an imposing façade adorned with fine statuary. The existing remains represent a reconstruction of the original and was built somewhat later than Paul's time but almost certainly follows the same lines and location. A long straight road runs from the theater to the harbor. In the city there was a magnificent agora with the usual surroundings of splendid buildings, temples, colonnades and a library. A monumental gateway led to the harbor.

A later and most impressive ruin at Ephesus is that of the double church of the Virgin Mary in which the Ecumenical Council of Ephesus was held A.D. 431. There are also extensive catacombs identified with the legend of the Seven Sleepers. According to this story seven Christians took refuge in the catacombs in the year 250 at the time of the Decian persecution. By order of the emperor the door of the cave was sealed and they were left to die. But instead of dying, they slept and were awakened two hundred years later when the stones were removed from the entrance. The sleepers, so it is said, reaffirmed their faith before the emperor Theodosius II and the Bishop Maxim and died about A.D. 450.

The last city to which Paul journeyed was Rome.* Its famous seven hills, varying in height from one hundred and fifty to four hundred and fifty feet, were seven ridges like spread fingers pointing to the Tiber. The city began on the flats and gradually spread to the nearby hills, much as Tehran is doing today. It was a city of teeming slums and beautiful pleasure palaces and government buildings, middle-class houses and the villas of the rich, gardens and lovely residences on the hills, truck farms on the flats and wharves along the river front. Like all ancient cities it was walled. In Paul's time the walls on three sides were five miles long, the river forming the fourth side. The walls were protected by an enormous trench, behind which were storerooms and barracks for the military. The Tiber itself was spanned by seven bridges, which were critical points in wartime.

Water for the city from mountain springs and streams was supplied by the famous aqueducts supported by graceful arches. The aqueducts brought water through seven portals and emptied into a hundred large reservoirs, which in turn fed seven hundred pools and five hundred fountains in public squares. They also supplied the luxurious public baths which were centers for relaxation, gossip and entertainment. Like other cities Rome had its large central forum, three hundred by one hundred and sixty feet, the size of a football field. At one end was a high rostrum, affording room for dignitaries during public assemblies. The forum was the religious, legal and commercial heart of the city. In addition, the city had many temples to many gods. Augustus is reported to have directed the repair of over eighty temples and innumerable shrines, altars and statues during his reign.

* Based on a description of Rome by Chester W. Quimby, *The Great Redemption* (New York: Macmillan, 1950).

There were two great open-air theaters, each seating twenty thousand. For mass athletics and gladiatorial combats there were the three great hippodromes, dedicated to Nero, Flaminius and Maximus. The Circus Maximus was seven hundred yards long and over a hundred yards wide; one circuit of the track was nearly a mile. It probably seated up to two hundred thousand spectators. There were memorial arches to Augustus and Tiberius and over three hundred statues of great and now-forgotten men, the famous and the infamous. In Paul's day a favored style of ornamentation was the decorated column; in Rome there were some four hundred columns of this sort in many small gardens and parks—truly a city deserving to be called the capital of the world.

But there were, as well, vast slums with crooked alleys and four- and five-storied buildings. There were many incidents of falling walls, collapsing floors and destructive fires, even as there are in Rome today. The only fire-fighting equipment consisted of bucket lines from the nearest fountain. The fire brigade was paid by the owners of the property involved. The owners had to bargain with the fire fighters before they would consent to put out the fire. If terms were not agreed on, the fire fighters withdrew and let the building burn. There was no system of garbage collection; the narrow streets were filled with decaying refuse. The large, stagnant moats about the city were excellent breeding grounds for mosquitoes; it is not surprising that epidemics were so frequent. The streets were not lighted at night, and robberies were of common occurrence in spite of the body of seven thousand policemen on night duty. With the exception of government chariots, equivalent to our "official cars," no vehicles were allowed on the streets in the daytime; the nights were made hideous by the incessant rumbling of delivery wagons and the shrill squeaking of the wheels. The traffic or trade of the city is vividly pictured in Revelation 18:10–13, the list of merchandise ending with "sheep and horses and chariots and slaves, and souls of men."

A proverb has it that all roads lead to Rome, and the Roman roads of the time were easily among the finest ever built. Paul entered Rome on the Appian Way, one of the most famous of arteries. It originally ran from Rome to Capua and was later extended to Brundisium. Some portions of it are even now in use. A Roman road usually consisted of four layers: at the bottom were flat stones laid in mortar, then rubble masonry of coarse concrete, a layer of fine concrete and, on top, cut stone polygons carefully fitted together. In some places the road was as much as three feet thick. We can imagine Paul's experience as he traveled along this famous highway, saw the converging traffic as it approached the world's capital and the graceful aqueduct paralleling the road, and finally glimpsed the distant shrines and villas on the tops of the hills of Rome.

The population of the city of Rome in Paul's day has been shown to be much greater than was once supposed. Historians had estimated the city to have contained around 1,200,000 persons, but in 1941 an inscription found at Ostia placed the population of Rome A.D. 14 as being 4,100,000. It was indeed a mighty city.

Most of the buildings and arches which Paul saw have long since crumbled into ruin, but a few landmarks of his day still stand. The most prominent of the ruins in the old forum is a portion of the temple dedicated to Castor and Pollux. Three beautiful pillars of that temple are still standing. On the southwest side of Palatine Hill is a building known as the Paedogogium, which is probably a portion of the ancient palace of the emperors. On its walls are many crude drawings. One of these is a caricature of a man with a huge donkey's head hanging on a cross. To one side stands another man with arms outstretched in the attitude of devotion. Underneath are the words: *Alexamenos Worships His God*. There can be little doubt that this is a mockery of the Christian religion; the cartoon dates from about A.D. 150.

Nearby one can see standing eight pillars of the old temple of Saturn. Close to the temple was a golden milepost, the Miliarium Aureum, on which was recorded a list of the greatest cities of the empire together with their distances from Rome. The names of both Jerusalem and London are said to have been among them, emphasizing Rome's proud position as the center of the ancient world. On the west of the forum are extensive remains of the Basilica Julia, dedicated by Julius Caesar in 46 B.C. and completed about A.D. 12. The basilica is of special interest to us because Paul probably stood in this building to hear the death sentence pronounced against him.

A short distance away and under the present church of San Giuseppe de Falegnami is a prison known as the Carcer Mamertinus. It is of two stories, the upper room vaulted, the lower a cubicle cut from solid rock to which the only entrance in Paul's day was through a hole in the floor of the upper room. The prison was described by Sallust around 50 B.C. and appears to have been exactly as it looks today. Many famous prisoners, including Vercingetorix and the confederates of Cataline in his conspiracy, were at one time or another confined here to wait their execution. Tradition says it was here that Paul was imprisoned; if so, it must have been at a later time than that mentioned in the Book of Acts, for there we read of his being in his own house and free to receive visitors. It is thought that Paul was freed at his first trial and went to Spain; he returned and was executed after a second trial at the time of the Neronian persecution. Clement, bishop of Rome from about A.D. 88 to about 97, says that Paul, "after he had been seven times in bonds, had been driven into exile, had been stoned, had been a preacher in the East and West, received the noble reward of his faith" (i.e., martyrdom). Clement wrote that both Paul and Peter were persecuted and contended unto death. Tertullian, writing about A.D. 200, says that under Nero "Paul obtained a birth suited to Roman citizenship when in Rome he sprang to life again ennobled by martyrdom," and of the church at Rome, "How happy is its church on which apostles poured forth all their doctrines along with their blood; where Peter endures a passion like his Lord's, where Paul wins his crown in a death like John's."

The strikingly different tone of Paul's last letter to Timothy and his other prison letters to the Philippians, Colossians, Ephesians and Philemon, would bear out the supposition of two imprisonments. In his letter to the Philippians, Paul writes that he feels sure of a speedy release and of visiting them again, but in his second letter to Timothy he seems to have written his own epitaph: "For I am now ready to be offered, and the time of my departure is at hand. I have fought a good fight, I have finished my course, I have kept the faith. Henceforth there is laid up for me a crown of righteousness, which the Lord, the righteous judge, shall give me at that day; and not to me only, but unto all them also that love his appearing."

An ancient tradition has it that Paul was buried near the Appian Way at a spot now marked by the imposing cathedral of St. Paul Without the Walls. The *Liber Pontificalis* says that Constantine directed that a basilica be built over the grave of Paul, and adds: ". . . and laid there the coffin with the body of the holy Paul . . ." and over the body "he set a cross of purest gold weighing 150 lbs. . . ."* The basilica was pillaged by the Saracens, and was acciden-

* Quoted in Finegan, *op. cit.*, p. 419.

tally destroyed by fire in 1823. Immediately after the last conflagration a new church was begun under Pope Leo XII; it was dedicated in 1854. A forecourt with granite columns was added in 1929. When the present church was being constructed it was possible to see under the high altar a marble slab on which was carved in Roman letters characteristic of the time of Constantine the words *Paulo Apostolo Martyri*. There is every reason to believe that beneath the slab rests the remains of Paul, the devoted slave of Christ.

An ancient tradition relates that Paul and Peter were martyred on the same day in Rome. Peter, a Roman citizen, was ordered beheaded; Paul was crucified. There has been much dispute as to whether this tradition has a basis in fact. To judge by the last chapter of Paul's final epistle, 2 Timothy, Peter was not in Rome at the close of Paul's life. Paul records that he is waiting the martyr's crown, and says, "Only Luke is with me." Had Peter been there, certainly he would have been mentioned.

The great cathedral of St. Peter's is built over the reputed site of Peter's martyrdom. Beginning in 1939, excavations were commenced under the floor of the cathedral in an attempt to discover his grave. Below the altar of the cathedral are the remains of the memorial built by the Emperor Constantine; below that, still another memorial, built about A.D. 160, to which the priest Gaius refers, who wrote at the end of the second century, "I can show you the trophies of the apostles. For whether you go to the Vatican or along the Ostian Way you will find the trophies of those who founded the church of Rome." Beneath this memorial was found a space in which were the bones of an elderly man of powerful physique, but it cannot be called a grave. Pope Pius XII has said that it is impossible to identify these bones as those of St. Peter, but there are many who believe that they are.

There is no evidence that before the end of the second century A.D. Christians took special care to preserve relics and burial places; the likelihood that the bones of Peter have been preserved is not great. It is more doubtful that it would have been possible for Christians under the terror of Nero's persecutions to possess themselves of the body of their martyred leader. It seems probable that the second-century monument was erected near the spot where he was believed crucified. The exact location of Peter's death, if indeed it was in Rome, as well as the significance of the bones uncovered beneath the memorial, must remain in doubt.

# 20

# THE SEVEN CHURCHES OF REVELATION

IN THE EARLY CHAPTERS OF THE BOOK OF REVELATION ARE THE LETTERS written by John to seven of the churches in western Asia Minor. Let us take a look at these cities and see what archeology has been able to discover of the cities as they were and the suitability of the messages addressed by John to each.

The first of these cities is Ephesus. We have discussed in some detail the establishment there of the Christian church in our references to Paul's third missionary journey. Let us note briefly the subsequent history of the Ephesian church. Historians tell us that it was subsequently governed by Timothy and by John and was acclaimed for its saints and martyrs. Tradition has it that Mary, the mother of Jesus, spent her last years nearby, cared for by Saint John. Gothic invaders destroyed both the famous temple to Diana and the great city itself A.D. 262. Later Ephesus was rebuilt and became a stronghold of Christianity. In the year 413, a general church council was held there to condemn Nestorius, bishop of Constantinople, the spiritual founder of the Nestorian church of Iran. One point Nestorius disputed was the decision to call Mary the "mother of God." When the council decided that Mary should be so called, there was tumultuous rejoicing in the city.

The decline of Ephesus seems to have been gradual. Malaria sapped the vitality of the people, and the city dwellers left the pestilential river and moved to higher ground. The river silt gradually filled up the harbor and the city became a marsh. The site of the temple was buried deep in mud, apparently by a flood. In the

Book of Revelation 2:5, John warns that unless the church in Ephesus repent and renew its former good works its "candlestick" will be taken away. If the word is thought of as a symbol of good fortune, it would seem that John's warning went unheeded. Surely, the city died.

Smyrna, fifty miles north of Ephesus, disputed with that city the right to the title of temple warden and guardian of the new religion. Christ, as one who was dead and came back to life, is a fitting God for the people of Smyrna, a city which was destroyed by the Lydians in the fifth century B.C. and rebuilt after four hundred years, thus returning to life. Pagos, a steep hill surmounted by stately public buildings, with the rest of the beautiful city spread along its slopes, has made the epithet "the crown of Smyrna" familiar to all. On coins the city is represented as a figure wearing a mural crown. The promise to the city of Smyrna in Revelation 2:10 is most appropriate: "I will give you a crown of life." Smyrna was famous for athletic contests and games where crown garlands were awarded the victors; the crown of life offered by Jesus was imperishable.

A Christian church existed in Smyrna from very early times, apparently originating in the large Jewish colony. Its most famous and most beloved bishop was Polycarp, a friend and pupil of Saint John. Polycarp loved to recall what he had been taught and the stories John had told him of the Master. He was over eighty years old when he undertook the journey to Rome in order to discuss the correct date for the celebration of Easter. He was received with signal honors by the Roman bishop Anicetus. Shortly after his return to Smyrna, persecution of Christians in that region grew more virulent. Polycarp, at the entreaty of friends, took refuge at a farm nearby.

A great festival was in progress in Smyrna; as a part of the celebration, eleven Christians were thrown to the lions in the amphitheater. Inflamed by the spectacle, the mob shouted for the blood of Polycarp and cried, "Away with the atheist!" Under torture a slave revealed the hiding place of the saintly old man. He was seized and the next day brought to the arena. The crowd howled at seeing him and demanded his death. Anxious to save the old man, the proconsul urged him to recant: "Swear by the genius of the emperor and say, 'Away with the atheists.'" Polycarp, looking gravely at the shouting mob, replied, "Away with the atheists." The proconsul urged him once more: "Swear, and I will release you. Revile him, revile your Christ." Polycarp replied: "Eighty and six years have I served him, and He has never wronged me. How can I blaspheme Him now, my King who saved me?"

The Asiarch Philip was asked to order Polycarp thrown to the lions. He refused, saying the games had ended. The mob took the law into its own hands, seized the old man, piled faggots about him and set him afire. The wind blew the flames so that they seemed to make an arch over his head and left him unharmed; whereupon the crowd demanded that the executioner run him through with a sword, and so Polycarp died in the arena. The city of Smyrna, albeit with many vicissitudes, remains to this day, the scene of the martyrdom of Polycarp. It is now known as Izmir.

The city of Pergamum was where official authority resided. Here, Christ was described as "he that hath the two-edged sword," the intention being to appeal to the city's respect for authority. Here was the first temple in all Asia to be dedicated to the worship of the Roman emperor; hence the city is described in the Book of Revelation as one "where Satan's throne is." In Revelation 2:13 men are warned that they must choose between the name of the emperor and the name of Christ. The meaning of a reference to a white stone is still a matter of dispute, not because no appropriate significance has been found but because too many possible parallels in the customs of Pergamum can be cited to explain it. It may have reference to the white stone which jurors used to voice their belief in the innocence of a man accused; it may refer to the stone tablet used as a "ticket" of admission to a banqueting hall; it may refer to the stones Urim and Thummin; it may refer to magic talismans used to gain entry to a fabled treasure cave.

To the faithful a promise is made, "I will give of the hidden manna," a reference to the manna which kept from starvation the Children of Israel as they wandered in the wilderness. In the Book of Revelation it means that those who abstain from forbidden meats will be fed with the spiritual bread of heaven.

Excavations conducted at Pergamum late in the nineteenth century resulted in the discovery of an altar to Zeus erected about 180 B.C. Found were carvings in high relief, the finest surviving from the school of Pergamene. On the top of a thousand-foot hill were temples to Zeus, to Soter, to Athena and to Dionysius. In the city was a temple to Aesculapius; a school of medicine once flourished in Pergamum.

The city of Thyatira was about forty miles southwest of Pergamum. Inscriptions show it to have been the headquarters for a number of strong and powerful trade guilds, and evidently their power endangered the growing Christian church and set against it the worship of idols. At meetings of the guilds, food which had been dedicated to idols was served, and in many ways the guilds acknowledged their awe and fear of heathen deities. The banquets of the guilds frequently ended in drunkenness and licentiousness, and as such the influence constituted a threat to the morality of the church. In the Book of Revelation is found a stern warning against the jezebels who seduce God's people and tempt them to eat meat sacrificed to idols. Fine brasswork was made in the bazaars of Thyatira, hence the description chosen, likening the Son of God to one "who hath eyes like unto a flame of fire and feet like fine brass."

Sardis, the former capital of Lydia, was thirty-five miles southwest of Thyatira. It was notorious for its gross immorality. The threat that Christ would come on them "as a thief in the night" was appropriate to this fortress, which twice in its history had been captured as a result of the carelessness of its defenders. Sardis was captured by Cyrus the Great when Croesus failed to garrison it properly; and Antiochus the Great took the fortress when his men succeeded in climbing the precipice, deemed unscalable and left unwatched. Christ commands the church: *Be Watchful.*

Philadelphia was twenty-eight miles southwest of Sardis. The city had been shaken once by a violent earthquake and the people had fled it in terror. Hence in Revelation is the demand that Christians of the city be as unshakable pillars. Following the earthquake, the city was named *Neo Caesarea* in gratitude for Caesar's help during the emergency. The believer, the Book of Revelation says, will be given by Christ "the name of my God, the name of the city of my God, and I will write upon him a new name and he shall go out from the city no more." It was the custom that the priest of the cult of the emperor, after his year in office, erect a statue in the temple on which would be written his name, that of his father, his place of birth and the year of his office. It remained as a perpetual memorial to his priesthood. Even so, says the New Testament, should the faithful stand in the temple of the true God. Because the city was in a vine-growing district, it is not surprising that the chief cult was the worship of Dionysius, the god of wine. Nevertheless, the Revelation of St. John the Divine clearly indicates, the Christian church in that city was one of high character, neither vexed by heresy nor contaminated by heathen practices, offering an open door, the door of missionary opportunity to all who believed.

Lukewarm—neither hot nor cold—is an apt description of the waters of some of the springs near Laodicea. John voices Christ's complaint against the people of Laodicea, who were apt to say "I am rich" as a sign of their complacency. It is not surprising that it should have been said at this center of banking. The city was famed for its prosperity and its obliviousness to matters of the spirit. Christ, through John, warns the people that they lack true riches, white garments rather than their famous black cloth, and spiritual eye salve rather than the ointment for which the city was renowned.

John's epistles to the churches were in no sense a form going out to all indiscriminately; instead, they were a compilation of individual letters, each wonderfully suited to the state of the Christian church in a specific place, and to the notable features of each city's physical and social environment, admirably designed to make personal the teachings of Christ and carrying admonitions and warnings most needed by each.

# CONCLUSION

THERE CAN BE NO CONCLUSION TO OUR SURVEY OF THE MAGNIFICENT panorama of history as it is contained in the Bible and enriched by the findings of archeology. To a degree that once would have been deemed incredible, the careful accuracy of the Bible picture has been repeatedly confirmed. The scholar, Dr. Nelson Glueck, after many years of study and personal exploration of the Holy Land, has this to say: "As a matter of fact . . . it may be stated categorically that no archaeological discovery has ever controverted a Biblical reference. Scores of archaeological findings have been made which confirm in clear outline or in exact detail historical statements in the Bible."* It can be confidently stated that although the primary purpose of Biblical writers was not to compose a history, their writings as an historical source are absolutely first class. Apart from their value as a profession of divine guidance, these several accounts are what we have come to expect of men witnessing to the deeds of the God of Truth whom they worshiped.

Much study remains to be done, and doubtless many additional discoveries will be made in the years to come; still it is clear that the extreme, critical view which calls for very late dates in the composition of many books of the New Testament will have to be abandoned. As we have seen, fragments of the Gospel of John have been found from a surprisingly early date, and in far-off places. Since the Qumran finds have revealed that the ideas and theological expressions of the Gospel were common property even before the

* Nelson Glueck, *Rivers in the Desert* (New York: Farrar, Straus and Cudahy, 1959), p. 31.

time of Christ, and are not, as has been argued, the final result of a
century and more of Christian reflection, the case for a late date is
of no import, indeed, is valueless. Besides, John's geographical accuracy and his intimate knowledge of Jerusalem as it was before
its fall demand an early and accurate source of information and
argue for an early date. Dr. Albright, recognized as the world's
archeological authority on both the Old Testament and the New
Testament, says: "In short, thanks to the Qumran discoveries, the
New Testament proves to be in fact what it was formerly believed
to be: the teaching of Christ and his immediate followers between
cir. 25 and cir. 80 A.D."† And, naturally, the closer we find a re-
porter to have been to the events he describes, the more confidence
we can place in his reports.

Biblical students everywhere are deeply indebted to the great
throng of archeologists who, with infinite pains and care, have uncovered some of the secrets of the past. And it is exhilarating to
realize what a great and promising future lies before them with the
advance of the science of archeology. In the Near East there are
literally thousands of mounds that have not been excavated, each
possibly containing uncountable secrets that one day may be revealed. With deep gratitude for all they have done, we wish them
well as they continue their studies and excavations.

Tehran, Iran                                         JOHN ELDER

† Albright, *From the Stone Age to Christianity*, p. 23.

# INDEX